ANSWERS TO COMMON
QUESTIONS ABOUT

Jesus

ANSWERS TO COMMON QUESTIONS ABOUT

Jesus

H. Wayne House
Timothy J. Demy

Kregel
Publications

Answers to Common Questions About Jesus
© 2011 by H. Wayne House and Timothy J. Demy

Published by Kregel Publications, a division of Kregel, Inc.,
P.O. Box 2607, Grand Rapids, MI 49501.

The views expressed in this book are solely those of the authors and do not represent or reflect the position or endorse-
ment of any governmental agency or organization, military
or otherwise.

Library of Congress Cataloging-in-Publication Data
House, H. Wayne.
    Answers to common questions about Jesus / H. Wayne
House and Timothy J. Demy.
        p. cm.
1. Jesus Christ—Person and offices—Miscellanea. 2. Bible—
Miscellanea. I. Demy, Timothy J. II. Title.
BT203.H68   2011   232—dc23   2011027523

ISBN 978-0-8254-2654-4

Printed in the United States of America

11 12 13 14 15 / 5 4 3 2 1

Contents

About This Series

The Answers to Common Questions series is designed to provide readers a brief summary and overview of individual topics and issues in Christian theology. For quick reference and ease in studying, the works are written in a question and answer format. The questions follow a logical progression so that those reading straight through a work will receive a greater appreciation for the topic and the issues involved. The volumes are thorough, though not exhaustive, and can be used as a set or as single volume studies. Each volume is fully documented and contains a recommended reading list for those who want to pursue the subject in greater detail.

The study of theology and the many issues within Christianity is an exciting and rewarding endeavor. For two thousand years, Christians have proclaimed the gospel of Jesus Christ and sought to accurately define and defend the doctrines of their faith as recorded in the Bible. In 2 Timothy 2:15, Christians are exhorted: "Be diligent to present yourself approved to God as a workman who does not need to be ashamed, accurately handling the word of truth." The goal of these books is to help you in your diligence and accuracy as you study God's Word and its influence in history and thought through the centuries.

Introduction

Jesus is the most important person in history. He has been the subject of movies and musicals, prose and poetry, dialogue and debates. Historians, artists, theologians, scientists, philosophers, lawyers, and journalists have studied Jesus. He has been called a revolutionary and a redeemer, a messiah and a maniac, a teacher and a preacher. There is no shortage of opinions about Jesus—some of them are accurate and based upon the biblical text and some are not. There are many views of Jesus, both secular and religious, Christian and non-Christian, informed and uninformed. Our goal in this brief work is to answer some of the most common questions about the person and work of Jesus of Nazareth.

In the final verse of the gospel of John, the author declared: "And there are also many other things which Jesus did, which if they were written in detail, I suppose that even the world itself would not contain the books that would be written" (John 21:25). Without a doubt, John's declaration is true, for the things that we do know about Jesus from the four gospel accounts have generated thousands of writings and books throughout the centuries.

With so many books, so many ideas, and so many opinions about Jesus, it is important to have a basic understanding about the life and work of Jesus. Evangelical theologian Carl F. H. Henry astutely declared that "the controversy over the person of Christ turns repeatedly through the centuries on much the same issues, so that one need only exchange names and times and places in the history of unbelief."[1] Whether one looks at the dialogues with Jesus recorded in the Gospels, the debates about Jesus in the first centuries of the Christian era, or the declarations about Jesus in contemporary culture, the issues are indeed much the same. Who was Jesus, what did He do, and why does it matter (or does it matter)? Join us as we look at common questions about Jesus—some of the answers have eternal consequences!

PART 1

The Life and Ministry of Jesus

1. When was Jesus born?

The biblical account does not give an exact date for the birth of Jesus, but many wrongly assume that He was born in A.D. 1, making the birth of Jesus the beginning of our current calendar. This would seem to make sense except for the fact that our calendar is different from the calendar used in the days of Jesus. Our dating comes from the calendar created by a monk by the name of Dionysius at the request of Pope John I in A.D. 525. Dionysius developed his chronology from the Roman reckoning of the founding of Rome 754 years prior to the beginning of the new Christian calendar. Thus 754 A.U.C. (*anno urbis conditae*) became A.D. 1. The years before the birth of Christ were called B.C., before Christ, and the year of His birth and afterward were called A.D., the year of our Lord (*anno Domini*). Unfortunately, Dionysius was inaccurate in his calculations. We now know that the death of Herod was 750 A.U.C., and the time of Christ's birth given in the gospel of Matthew occurred before this event. Consequently, Jesus must have been born before 4 B.C. under our current calendar.[1]

With this date as our last possible date for the birth of Jesus, when might be the earliest time for His birth? We know from the gospel of Luke that the birth of Jesus occurred after a decree from Caesar Augustus that the Roman world was to be enrolled for purposes of taxation. Augustus reigned from 44 B.C. to A.D. 14 (no year 0 is between 1 B.C. and A.D. 1), but this is of little help. It is necessary to narrow the range, but Luke also provides this for us. He mentions that this registration occurred when Quirinius governed Syria. Some have questioned this census, since Quirinius governed several years later than the death of Herod. It is now known, however, that two censuses were taken in two periods of Quirinius's governance. Romans held a census every fourteen years beginning with Augustus. One was in 23–22 B.C. and another in 9–8 B.C. It is the latter of which Luke writes. Quirinius was governor two times, in 7 B.C. and in A.D. 6. The procedure for the taking of a Roman census has been discovered from a papyrus in Egypt: "The enrollment by household being at hand, it is necessary to notify all who for any cause soever are outside their homes to return to their domestic hearths. . . ."[2]

Was Jesus born December 25? This is a tradition of Western Christianity (January 6 was held by the Eastern Church), but there is no certainty of this date in early Christianity.[3] Some question the likelihood of the birth occurring in the winter in Bethlehem. It might be considered unlikely since sheep are said not to be in the fields during the winter but in the sheepfold due to the cold weather. Considerable evidence exists, however, that indicates sheep were not allowed in the wilderness during the winter but around Bethlehem this was permissible. Also, the winters are often mild so that this would not be a problem. The shepherds, then, could easily have been watching their sheep in a mild December or January when the announcement from the angelic host caused them to go to visit the young child in a cave in Bethlehem. We agree with the important study of Harold Hoehner that places Jesus' birth no earlier than December of 6 B.C. (probably in 5) or January of 4 B.C.[4]

2. Where was Jesus born?

The birthplace of Jesus as Bethlehem (Luke 2:4) would appear to be an easy answer for anyone reading the Bible, but a problem arises in that there were two Bethlehems in ancient Israel. The one with which most of us are familiar is Bethlehem of Judea, approximately six miles south of Jerusalem. The other Bethlehem is Bethlehem of Galilee, about ten miles from Nazareth. Mary and Joseph lived in Nazareth, so that many believe that the latter Bethlehem would be the place to which they would travel. This alternative Bethlehem was also known as Bethlehem of Zebulun, to distinguish it from Bethlehem of Judea. The name Bethlehem means "house of bread."

In evaluating the two views, one is immediately struck with the clear teaching of both the Hebrew and Christian Scriptures as they speak of Messiah being born in Bethlehem of Judea. For example, the prophet Micah says, "But as for you, Bethlehem Ephrathah, too little to be among the clans of Judah, from you One will go forth for Me to be ruler in Israel. His goings forth are from long ago, from the days of eternity" (Micah 5:2). It was necessary that Messiah be born in the land of Judea in Bethlehem, and not in Galilee. Matthew records these words of Micah as being fulfilled in the life of Jesus, "Now after Jesus was born in Bethlehem of Judea in the days of Herod the king, magi from the east arrived in Jerusalem. . . . They said to him [Herod], 'In Bethlehem of Judea; for this is what has been written by the prophet: "AND YOU, BETHLEHEM, LAND OF JUDAH, ARE BY NO MEANS LEAST AMONG THE LEADERS OF JUDAH; FOR OUT OF YOU SHALL COME FORTH A RULER WHO WILL SHEPHERD MY PEOPLE ISRAEL"'" (Matt. 2:1, 5–6).

Secondly, Joseph is seen to be of the line of David the king in the genealogies of Matthew and Luke; thus, he is of the tribe of Judah, and not of Zebulun, so it was necessary for him to enroll in the city of David, Bethlehem of Judea. Third, the natural reading of the story of the wise men and Herod is for a locality near Jerusalem. The wise men went to the city of Bethlehem of Judea.

Luke's account of the birth of Christ has Joseph going to Judea for the enrollment required by the decree of Caesar Augustus (Luke 2:1, 4). The account of the shepherds in Judea makes more sense than having shepherds in Galilee, which was farmland rather than the hill country of Judea where sheepherding was the standard.

John 7:42 recounts a story in which those challenging Jesus had difficulty understanding how He was Messiah since He lived in Galilee, and yet they knew from Micah 5:2 that the Messiah was to be born in Bethlehem of Judea. It was a natural confusion for them and, because of this, they did not understand Him to be who He was.

Finally, some have argued that such a strenuous journey on a donkey from Nazareth to Bethlehem of Judea is unlikely since this would have been too much for a pregnant woman of nine months and might even cause a miscarriage. The first thing to notice is that the biblical text does not say Joseph and Mary traveled by donkey; people have been looking at pictures of this too long and not reading the text. Second, the seventy- to ninety-mile trek, depending on the route, probably would have been made over a number of days, even a week or more, so it would not have been as strenuous as sometimes thought. We forget the kind of journeys that many people took across America in the nineteenth century in similar situations. Additionally, Joseph and Mary probably would not have traveled alone but rather in some kind of caravan. They could also have stopped along the way to stay with relatives. The text is plain, and so there is no need to force the text to mean something else or to invent stories. Jesus was born in Bethlehem of Judea, the birthplace and original home of King David from the Old Testament (1 Sam. 16:1–13; 17:12).

3. What is the meaning of the name Jesus?

The English word *Jesus* is a transliteration of the Greek *Iesous* or Latin *Iesus*, from the Hebrew word *Yeshua'*, meaning "Yahweh saves," a later form found in the New Testament period of the earlier *Yehoshua'* (Joshua), meaning "Yahweh is salvation." This Hebrew word is used throughout the Hebrew Scriptures as a word for physical and spiritual salvation, deliverance, help, or security. The name was known and used throughout biblical times, but only with the birth of Jesus of Nazareth was the meaning of the name truly fulfilled. When the angel visited Mary to inform her that she was God's choice to be the mother of Messiah, he spoke these words, "She will bear a Son; and you shall call His name *Yeshua* [Jesus] for He will save His people from their sins" (Matt. 1:21).[5]

4. Who were Jesus' siblings?

We know little of most of Jesus' siblings other than James and Judas (Jude), but Matthew 13:55–56 indicates that He had other brothers and sisters: "'Is not this the carpenter's son? Is not His mother called Mary, and His brothers, James and Joseph and Simon and Judas? And His sisters, are they not all with us? Where then did this man get all these things?'"

There is no evidence that any of His brothers or sisters believed in Him as the Messiah during His early life or His ministry on earth. In fact, John 7:2–6 shows that Jesus' brothers taunted Him and the text says that they did not believe in Him (v. 5). Mark 6:4 indicates that the rejection of Jesus occurred within His own household. Since this would clearly not include Joseph and Mary, the comment would refer to His siblings. A further indication of this unbelief among the brothers occurred at the cross, where Jesus, the oldest son, committed the care of His mother to His cousin John rather than His younger brothers (John 19:25–27).

Fortunately, the story does not end here because after the resurrection we know that James had a personal visitation from the Lord Jesus (1 Cor. 15:7), and later he became leader of the Jerusalem church (Acts 15). His brothers and His mother were present in the upper room on the day of Pentecost (Acts 1:13–14), and Judas, whom we call Jude to distinguish him from the betrayer Judas, wrote a book of the New Testament.

Some Roman Catholics (as well as a few Protestants) argue that

Jesus did not have brothers and sisters and the word used for *brothers* means cousins (a view also held by Christian leaders in Egypt in the early third century). Yet, in each instance, the specific word for *brother* and not *cousin* is used. While the word can mean cousin, there is no lexical necessity for such usage in these instances. Some have also argued that Jesus' brothers and sisters were half brothers and half sisters who were the children of Joseph from an earlier marriage. There is no evidence for such a marriage in the biblical text. Arguments for Jesus not having brothers and sisters are tied to the later teaching of Roman Catholicism and Eastern Orthodoxy of the perpetual virginity of Mary.

5. Was Jesus ever married?

The idea that Jesus was married during His earthly existence stems from two divergent sources in general. The first source is from Latter-day Saints (Mormons), who have taught that Jesus was married, perhaps to more than one woman, namely, Mary of Magdala (Mary Magdalene) and possibly Mary and Martha. The wedding at Cana of Galilee is said to have been one of His weddings.[6] However, the text of John 2:2 says that Jesus was invited to this wedding, along with His mother, and certainly a bridegroom does not need such an invitation.

Early Latter-day Saint leader Orson Hyde also taught that the reference to Mary in the garden in which she says, "They have taken away my Lord" (John 20:13) is proof of their marriage, understanding Lord as husband. Certainly a wife might call her husband Lord, as Sarah did of Abraham (1 Peter 3:6), but Lord is used various ways in the New Testament, in no way indicating a marital relationship with the term. There is no basis for understanding the word as specifically signifying marriage in reference to Mary Magdalene, Mary, or Martha. The word is used of the virgins attending a wedding (Matt. 25:11) and the woman seeking assistance from Jesus (Mark 7:28). Nothing in the context for Mary and Martha in Luke 10:40–41 or Mary of Magdala in John 20:13, 18 shows any difference from other uses of the word *Lord* in the New Testament. Both men and women call Jesus Lord throughout the Gospels as either a title of respect, or sometimes equivalent to Yahweh (LORD) (cf. Luke 1:43; 2:11; 5:8, 12; 7:6).

The second source for saying Jesus was married comes from popular culture and pseudohistorians. Dan Brown, in the best-selling novel *The Da Vinci Code*, has argued through the character of Professor Teabing that Jesus was married to Mary Magdalene and had children. Part of the reason is Teabing's assertion that it was un-Jewish to be unmarried. This is not the case. Though it was customarily, there were many men in New Testament times who were not married, as evidenced by the community of Qumran, in which celibacy was practiced. If, in fact, Jesus were married, Paul the apostle (an unmarried Jew) missed an important opportunity to strengthen his argument in his first epistle to the Corinthians: "Do we not have a right to take along a believing wife, even as the rest of the apostles and the brothers of the Lord and Cephas?" (1 Cor. 9:5). This would have been a perfect place to use the marriage of Christ Jesus to support Paul's right of also having a wife.[7]

No passage in the biblical Gospels says or intimates that Jesus was married to anyone. Brown (and others) believe that there is support in an extrabiblical gospel of the second century known as the Gospel of Philip:

As for the Wisdom who is called "the barren," she is the mother of the angels. And the companion of the [. . .] Mary Magdalene. [. . .] loved her more than all the disciples, and used to kiss her often on her mouth. The rest of the disciples [. . .]. They said to him "Why do you love her more than all of us?" The Savior answered and said to them, "Why do I not love you like her? When a blind man and one who sees are both together in darkness, they are no different from one another. When the light comes, then he who sees will see the light, and he who is blind will remain in darkness."[8]

According to the novel, Jesus kissed Mary Magdalene on the mouth, bringing about jealousy from the apostles. Attached to this is the claim that the word *companion* speaks of a spouse. Both of these assertions from the novel are false. The text is actually worn through in the Gospel of Philip papyrus, so we don't know where Jesus kissed Mary according to this second-century Gnostic gospel; it may have been on the cheek. Additionally, Teabing declares that the word *companion* is an Aramaic word for spouse, but the Gospel of Philip is Coptic, not Aramaic, so his point is irrelevant.

There is simply no credible historical or textual evidence that Jesus was ever married; neither biblical documents nor heretical books support the idea.[9] Such a view finds support only in fictional and sensationalistic books. On the other hand, there are no moral or physical reasons why Jesus could not have married. Marriage is honorable in the sight of God and serves His purpose for filling the earth (Gen. 1:26–28) and representing His relationship with His people (Eph. 5). Moreover, Jesus was a true human and so was capable of marriage and propagation. As was the case with Paul, His task in this world was more focused, so marriage would have not been desirable. Jesus came into this world to serve and to save humanity, to die for us and not to enjoy the pleasures of being a husband and father.

6. Where did Jesus travel in His ministry?

Did Jesus travel to far lands or did he largely minister to the Jewish community of ancient first-century Israel? This question has been raised by recent claims that Jesus may have visited places like India (according to Hinduism and Damascus), southeastern Turkey, and maybe even Afghanistan (according to Islam).

In one tradition, in His early life Jesus received spiritual training from holy men in India and then returned to Jerusalem after His thirteenth birthday. Rather than dying later on the cross, He traveled back to India, finally dying and being buried in Kashmir. Another Indian view is that Jesus went to the East after His resurrection.

These accounts arose in the second century after A.D. 115, most likely after the preaching of Thomas in India in the first century when the story of Jesus became confused with local lore.[10] Also in the East, Buddhism came from Hinduism, and it appears that some of the stories about Jesus became combined with stories of Gautama Buddha. They are both said to have fasted for forty days, to have been tempted by Satan, to have referred to themselves as the light, and to have taught the love of enemies.

Finally, some traditions within Islam have Jesus going to Damascus in Syria for a period of two years about the time that Paul traveled toward Damascus. He is said also to have preached to the king of Nisibis in southeastern Turkey and in Afghanistan, where He performed miracles.

All of these accounts surfaced after the time of the New Testament and have little, if any, support for their credibility. They seem to have emerged because of the spread of the Gospel of Jesus in these parts of the world when confusion with the historical Jesus and the Gospel about Him occurred.

In the past two centuries, some authors have argued that there were "lost years" in the life of Jesus during which He traveled throughout the world to England and elsewhere. This seems to be based on two passages: John's statement in John 21:25 that there were many unrecorded activities of Jesus and the statement of John the Baptist in John 1:31. Neither of these verses, however, supports such an interpretation. John is referring to things Jesus did as part of His ministry in Palestine with His disciples. The comment of John the Baptist that he did not know Jesus makes sense in light of the fact that John the Baptist lived a reclusive life in the desert before beginning his public ministry (Luke 1:80).[11]

What do we really know of the travels of Jesus? We have specific statements about travel in His early life before being declared as God's Messiah. As a baby He went to Egypt with His mother and father, and then to Nazareth after Herod the Great's death in A.D. 4. During His ministry He visited different parts of the land of Israel, such as the lake of Galilee and cities around this lake. Bethsaida and modern Kursi, the place of the casting out of demons into pigs, are two such cities. He went to Cana, where He turned the water into wine. He took His disciples to Caesarea Philippi (ancient Panias and modern Banias). He preached in the cities of Tyre and Sidon in southern Lebanon. John was baptizing beyond the Jordan, so Jesus traveled on the other side of the Jordan in modern Jordan to be baptized. Though some believe that Jesus was transfigured at Mt. Tabor, this amazing event probably took place on Mt. Hermon (in Lebanon) since what are called mountains in Israel are really hills, and the only real "high" mountain mentioned in the New Testament is Mt. Hermon.

It is also clear that Jesus went to Jerusalem a number of times, the final time during His ministry being the week of His passion. Since He was an observant Jew, He would have traveled to the various Jewish feasts, especially Passover, Pentecost, and the Feast of Tabernacles, as well as the Feast of Dedication. This would have required Him to travel from Capernaum (His home) to Jerusalem several times each year.

7. When did Jesus die?

Biblical scholars have debated the exact year of Jesus' death and suggested many options. Depending upon the credibility of the sources used to determine the date of His death, proposed years have ranged from A.D. 21 to A.D. 36.[12] The extreme date of A.D. 21 is based upon the apocryphal work known as *Acts of Pilate*, and can be rejected because it is before the dates of the officials of the trial, Caiaphas the high priest and the Roman Prefect Pontius Pilate, who served concurrently between the years A.D. 26 and A.D. 36. Most commentators hold to a date between A.D. 30 and A.D. 33. For several reasons, we believe that an A.D. 33 date is the most probable.

Based upon a study of the harmonization of the four gospels with regard to the different calendars used to reckon the date of Passover by various Jewish groups and geographical regions, the probable day and time of Jesus' death was the fourteenth day of the Jewish month Nisan at 3 P.M.[13] The Jewish month was a lunar month of twenty-nine to thirty days. A review of the astronomical evidence for the range of years established above of A.D. 26 to A.D. 36 shows that Nisan 14 occurred on a Friday four times: A.D. 27, 30, 33, and 36 (with the 27 date being possible but unlikely).[14] The A.D. 36 date is ruled out because there is no indication in the Gospels that the ministry of Jesus lasted six years. Luke 3:1–3 states that the ministry of John the Baptist began in the fifteenth year of the reign of Tiberius, which was A.D. 29. Since John the Baptist was a forerunner of Jesus, the ministry of Jesus began after A.D. 29, likely in the summer or autumn of A.D. 29.[15] That leaves two possible dates for the crucifixion, A.D. 30 and A.D. 33. If one accepts the beginning of John's ministry as A.D. 29 and accepts a three-year ministry span for Jesus as is commonly understood from the biblical text, then A.D. 33 becomes the most plausible year for the death of Jesus. We believe that when studied together, the biblical, historical, and astronomical records provide a specific date. Jesus died Friday, April 3, A.D. 33.

8. Where did Jesus die and rise again?

The place of Jesus' death, burial, and resurrection has been important to Christians for the last two thousand years. Though, certainly, the truth and meaning of these events is most important, the Christian faith (unlike many other world religions) is deeply tied to history. The Creator of the universe entered into His creation in the person of the Son in order to redeem all who would believe in the salvation He offered at the cross. Jesus Christ rose from the dead to demonstrate that He indeed was the Son of God who held power over death and could legitimately offer eternal life to those who believe on His name.

Since the reality of this offering from Jesus is dependent on the reality of His death in A.D. 30 or 33 (dependent on one's view), where did this crucifixion, burial, and resurrection occur? For most of the history of the church, there has been but one site considered the traditional place of the death, burial, and resurrection, located within the Church of the Holy Sepulchre. However, an alternate site began to be offered in the nineteenth century called Gordon's Calvary after British Major-General Charles Gordon (1833–1885). This site has been adopted as the authentic place of the Lord's death, burial, and resurrection. When one visits the traditional site of these events, housed in the Church of the Holy Sepulchre with all of its architecture, ornamentation, ceremony, and surroundings, as compared with the simplicity of Gordon's Calvary (also called the Garden Tomb) in the midst of a beautiful garden, a hillside slightly resembling a human skull, and a structure easily identified as a tomb, the latter alternative has become very appealing (especially to many Protestants).

Which of these two sites, if either, is the location of the extraordinary acts of Jesus between Friday and Sunday nearly two thousand years ago? What is required for a location to fit the biblical, archaeological, and historical evidence? The place of crucifixion is more difficult to determine, but it must be in close proximity to the tomb, as one of the requirements for the place of burial. Let us first examine Golgotha, the "Place of a Skull" (Matt. 27:33).

What is meant by the place of a skull? Is it necessary to find a hillside that looks like a skull? If so, then there is no evidence of such in the Church of the Holy Sepulchre, whereas the Garden Tomb has a hill (now a Muslim cemetery) with features that somewhat resemble a skull. This would seem to argue in favor of the Garden Tomb outside the current Old City. When the Scripture mentions Golgotha, the place of the skull, in Matthew 27:33, should we understand that the place of crucifixion looked like a skull, or that it was simply a designation for a place of crucifixion, a place where skulls and bones lay? The latter seems more likely, for a site with such an appearance dating back approximately two thousand would surely have borne some testimony by Christians, but there is none. If one observes the current state of this hill and compares it with pictures of approximately one hundred years ago, it becomes obvious that erosion has caused the possible resemblance to a skull, but would it have looked this way many hundreds of years ago, even at the time of Jesus? Biblical scholars and archaeologists are basically in agreement that the area has been dug out during mining in the quarry over the last few hundred years and its appearance is due to this, as well as natural causes.

What about the tomb in the Garden Tomb site as compared with the Church of the Holy Sepulchre? The church currently has no tomb of Christ but has instead a small chapel where the alleged tomb of Christ stood before being chiseled to the ground in the early eleventh century.[16] A number of conditions are required to satisfy the biblical account of the tomb of Christ:

1. It had to be near the site of the crucifixion.
2. It had to be located in a garden.
3. It had to be outside the city walls of Jerusalem when Jesus was crucified in the early A.D. 30s.
4. It had to be hewed out of a stone quarry.
5. It had to be an exceptional tomb since it was a rich man's tomb.
6. It had to have a rolling stone.
7. It had to have an outer chamber and inner chamber in view of the biblical accounts regarding the women, apostles, and angels at the tomb.
8. It had to be a new tomb, thus hewed in the first century A.D.

The Garden Tomb satisfies numbers 1–4, and 7–8. Item 5 is questionable since there are larger tombs than the small Garden Tomb. Item 6 is uncertain since a rolling stone was not found at the site; in addition, the trough in front of the Garden Tomb is not a groove for a rolling stone but is rather a water trough going all the way across the front of the tomb. Item 8 is the most significant since there is no doubt that the Garden Tomb is a First Temple–era tomb, created hundreds of years before Jesus and part of a quarry of eighth century B.C. tombs; consequently, it cannot be the correct tomb, since Jesus was placed in a newly created tomb. If the Church of the Holy Sepulchre is not the tomb of Christ, then we have no knowledge of where it is.

The Church of the Holy Sepulchre does not have many of the items of support that the Garden Tomb does due to the fact that the church and the tomb were destroyed in the early eleventh century by the order of Fatimid Caliph Al-Hakim bi-Amr Allah. Nonetheless, the tradition for this site is strong, going back to the early second century. Emperor Hadrian, attempting to eradicate Christianity and Judaism, built a temple to Venus over the site, a temple to Jupiter over the site of the destroyed Jewish temple, and a shrine to the mythological figure Adonis, the lover of the Greek goddess Aphrodite, at the Church of the Nativity, effectively marking these important sites for future generations. Church fathers attest that the Church of the Holy Sepulchre (known as Church of the Resurrection by the Greek Orthodox) was the place of the resurrection. Those items required for the actual place of Christ's tomb are also present at the Church of the Holy Sepulchre. It is near the site of crucifixion. A garden used to be present, according to archaeological investigation. It was outside the city walls when Jesus died, a wall being built approximately ten years later. It is located in a quarry that was used until the first century B.C. The small building that encases the tomb (in the fourth century the tomb was separated from the stone around it) is near tombs of the Second Temple period, and has an inner and outer chamber.

In recent years another burial site has been proposed by some, popularly known as "the Jesus Family Tomb" or "the Talpiot Tomb" (Talpiot, a suburb of Jerusalem). In the tomb were ossuaries (stone boxes containing bones) and, in brief, the hypothesis was that because of name similarities on some of the ossuaries to family members of Jesus, the tomb was the family tomb of Jesus. Also part of the claim was that one ossuary was that of Jesus. The sensational claims have been thoroughly refuted, but the idea is still prominent in media documentaries in popular culture. There are many shortcomings of the theory, but the greatest is that it requires that the resurrection of Jesus be a spiritual resurrection only and not a bodily resurrection. The hypothesis has no credibility. New Testament scholar Darrell Bock, who was personally involved in the evaluations of the claims, writes: "The fact that there is so little to this hypothesis and yet it gained so much attention and created so much hype raises the question of whether our culture truly is ready and willing to come to grips with the claims of Jesus as they have been made over the centuries."[17]

Though the location of Christ's place of death, burial, and resurrection is not known for certain, the evidence provides for the traditional site to be the correct place, long remembered in the minds of the early Christians and accepted by most Christians for nearly two thousand years.

9. How did the Gospels interpret Scripture regarding Jesus?

The apostles interpreted the Old Testament texts about the Messiah in the same way as the rabbis in the first century A.D., though they were more cautious in their methodology. The biblical texts were understood in four ways by the rabbis and the apostles:

1. The first and most prevalent method of interpretation is the *literal* approach, called *pshat*. For example, the gospel author Matthew interprets the birth of the Messiah in Bethlehem in Micah 5:2 as fulfilled in Matthew 2:5–6.

2. The second method of interpretation may be expressed as *typology*, called *remez*. Matthew 2:14–15 uses this approach. The exodus of the Hebrews from Egypt was a historical event and not a prophecy. So how did Matthew understand this event? He quoted Hosea 11:1, which says, "When Israel was

a youth I loved him, And out of Egypt I called My son." This was not a prophecy and Matthew knew this. The exodus of the Hebrews is a type of God calling Jesus, His greater Son, out of Egypt.

3. The third method is *drash*, in which the interpreter is focusing on only one point of connection between an original idea or event and applies an application of the truth from the original event to the new situation (*this is that*). For example, Herod murdered the male children in Bethlehem under age two years. Matthew sees this terrible act of Herod as similar to what was spoken by Jeremiah in Jeremiah 31:15 regarding the mourning of the women in Ramah. Rachel, mother of the Jewish people, stands for all of these Jewish mothers crying at the loss of their children being led away into captivity in Babylon, where they would see them no more. In similar fashion, these Jewish mothers who have lost their sons to the butchery of Herod would see their children no more. There is similarity in only one area, the great pain these mothers felt. This is not a literal interpretation but is an application of one point of comparison.

4. The fourth way in which the biblical text was understood is called *sod*, meaning secret, in which various biblical texts teaching a particular idea are drawn together in summary form to teach a truth. Matthew 2:22–23 is an example, where Matthew says, ". . . and came and lived in a city called Nazareth. That was to fulfill what was spoken through the prophets: 'He shall be called a Nazarene.'" One cannot find such a statement in the Old Testament. Rather than reference a particular biblical text, the interpreter draws together and summarizes biblical truth found in passages of the Old Testament. When one examines several passages in the Old Testament about the Messiah, it is discoverd that the Messiah would be hated and then rejected by His own people (John 1:11), similar to the rejection of the Nazarenes.[18]

10. What languages did Jesus speak?

Until the last few decades, it was routinely argued that Jesus spoke Aramaic as His native tongue, but it is recognized today that Hebrew also was a spoken language in the land of Israel during the time of Jesus. When the Babylonians, who spoke Aramaic, conquered the Jewish people in the sixth century B.C., they did not take all the people of Israel into captivity. Those who went into exile in Babylon acquired Aramaic as their major language, but the people who remained behind continued to use Hebrew as well as Aramaic, the lingua franca (working language) in that part of the world at that time. There are many surviving Aramaic inscriptions, even around Jerusalem, so we know that this language still had an impact on the nation in the time of Jesus, but we also have much in Hebrew. The scrolls at Qumran, which existed from the second century B.C. until approximately A.D. 70, exclusively used Hebrew in their sectarian documents, not to mention the Hebrew Scriptures they copied. Jesus most likely learned Hebrew and Aramaic, but what of other languages?

When Alexander the Great conquered the ancient Near East about 330 B.C., Greek began to be popularly spoken, even throughout Israel, but more so in the Galilee of the northern portion of the country. It remained a powerful force in the Galilee in which Jesus lived, and it is doubtful that He did not have at least familiarity with this language.

Last of all, the Romans came into Israel in 63 B.C., in order to resolve a dispute of warring parties, but never left. Their presence in the land naturally led to the Jewish and Greek people's exposure to Latin. Consequently, Jesus, as a Jew, would probably have been familiar with the Latin spoken by Roman soldiers. Moreover, He lived in Nazareth (where a Roman garrison was stationed), and this was also close to Seppharos, capital of the region of Galilee (later moved to Tiberias). It is thought that He and His stepfather, Joseph, probably worked in Seppharos. So Jesus would have come into regular contact with the Latin language.

So what languages did Jesus speak? He probably spoke both Hebrew and Aramaic regularly, and probably knew business and social words of Greek and Latin.

PART 2

The Person of Jesus According to the Bible

11. Where was Jesus before His birth?

To speak of Jesus, one must remember that He is unlike any person who has ever been in that He was an uncreated person who has existed from all eternity. He has life in Himself and, with the Father and the Holy Spirit, is the eternal, infinite God. The eternal Son of God took upon Himself full humanity without ceasing to be fully God. Several passages of Scripture give us insight into the preexistent Christ. The apostle John in his gospel begins with "In the beginning was the Word, and the Word was with God, and the Word was God" (John 1:1). This verse is pivotal to understanding the person of Jesus in reference to His deity. When the beginning happened—that is to say, at creation—Jesus already existed, meaning He never had a beginning. Next John says that Jesus, the Logos (Word), was with God before the incarnation (he talks of this in v. 14). The word *with*, though, speaks not merely of being together with someone or in the presence of someone; rather, the Greek word means "toward." Jesus faced the Father from all eternity, in close relationship. This is similar to the teaching in John 1:18, that the Son was in the bosom of the Father, and that He is the only-begotten God. This reminds us of the teaching of the Nicene Creed that says the Son is God of very God. The Son is begotten of the Father from all eternity but then takes upon Himself the creaturely nature of a human being in order to give Himself for us as a servant and a savior. Lest there be misunderstanding, John follows with the words that "the Word was God." He was before the beginning in fellowship with God (the Father, cf. 1 John) and He was God. All of this is before He became man. Jesus, in His prayer to the Father in John 17, emphasizes that He desired to be glorified by the Father with the glory that He had enjoyed with Him before the beginning of the world (John 17:5).

The apostle John continues in chapter 1 verse 3, "All things came into being through Him, and apart from Him nothing came into being that has come into being." This same thought is reiterated by Paul in Colossians 1:15–16, where he says that Jesus is the mirror image of God and the "first-bearer" (the concept in Greek) of all creation because all things were created by Him and for Him. Consequently, if the Son was the creator of everything that is not God, existing with the Father before creation (time, space, matter, as well as the spiritual realm, according to Col. 1:16), then obviously He was God as to His nature and the Son as to His person, before His birth.

This leads us to another issue, and that is when did Jesus become the Son of God? The biblical teaching is that He always was the Son of God, and did not become so in the birth through Mary. The Father gave His Son as Savior of the world; He did not give a generic person of the Godhead to become the Son of God by His birth, baptism, or resurrection. The Messiah spoken about in Isaiah 7:14, to be born of a virgin, is the same Son of Isaiah 9:6, who is the mighty God and Father of eternity before He took upon Himself humanity (Phil. 2:5ff.). He did not become Son at the baptism but rather was identified as the Son of God when He began His public ministry. And He did not become the Son of God at the resurrection, but according to Paul, He was declared the Son of God because of the resurrection. This becomes especially clear when Jesus identifies

Himself as "I AM" in John 8:58. Before Abraham came into existence (two thousand years earlier), He already was. Fourteen hundred years before the earthly Jesus was born, Moses encountered the I AM at Mt. Sinai. He had been observing the people of Israel in Egypt for nearly four hundred years (cf. Gen. 15) and heard their cries, so that He had come down to deliver them. This is Jesus—God with us—but now not in manifestations of power such as a burning bush, a fiery cloud, or parted sea; He has come as a man who will show us the way to a relationship to God through His suffering.

12. How does Jesus relate to the Trinity?

Jesus is not only a human in every respect, He is also fully God; consequently, He is one of the persons of the divine Trinity. The association of Jesus with the Father becomes plain in the New Testament, in which Jesus claims a relationship with the Father not open to any ordinary human. He was with the Father from all eternity (John 1:1). He was the creator of the universe (Col. 1:16–17). He and the Father share the same divine nature (John 10:30; Col. 2:9). These examples, and many more, may be set forth to demonstrate that Jesus is one God with the Father and the Holy Spirit.

What needs to be explained is how this relationship works out in what is known as the works within the Godhead and works outside the Godhead; our concern is with the former. How does the Son of God function within the Trinity, and how does the Son of God function along with the Father and Holy Spirit in relationship to creation? Let us look at the various works of the members of the Holy Trinity in relation to each other.

The three persons of the Trinity share the entire being of God without any separation, but they are distinct from each other. For example, whatever the Father knows or chooses as God is always what the Son and the Holy Spirit also knows or chooses. All of the attributes of God are equally the entire possession of each member of the Godhead, but how the persons relate to each other in the exercise of the attributes may vary. This is why all members of the

Trinity are involved in our salvation as God, but each member has a distinct relationship to that salvation: the Father chooses to save humanity and sends the Son; the Son comes into the world and gives Himself as a sacrifice; the Spirit comes from the Father and Son to convict, judge, and regenerate humans who are to be saved.

The Father begets the Son from all eternity. This means that the Son never came into existence and has been in relationship with the Father as His Son from eternity. Humans have difficulty in understanding a self-existent God who is the first cause for all of creation (all that is NOT God), including time, space, and all spiritual and physical reality. The Father shared glory with the Son before the world began and has loved the Son for all eternity. When the Father in eternity decreed or decided to save sinful humanity, in eternity He chose to send His Son to be the Savior (John 3:16). He did not send Jesus and then decide He would be Savior. He has always been the one who would be Savior and came into the creation to accomplish the task.

The Son is equal to the Father and Holy Spirit in every respect in regard to the attributes of the being of God and yet is relationally distinct from each of the persons. For example, the Father, Son, and Holy Spirit share the same omnipotence, but the Son is in submission to the Father relationally, and the Holy Spirit is sent by the Father through the Son, apparently under both. Again, this is only in reference to their intra-Trinitarian relationship and not to imply inferiority in any way as to their divine nature.

13. Did Jesus claim to be God?

The deity of Jesus the Messiah has been firmly believed since the inception of the Christian church. The confession of Peter at Caesarea Philippi—in which, by the revelation of the Father, he declared Jesus to be the Messiah, the Son of the living God (Matt. 16:16)—was later supported by him when he spoke of "the righteousness of our God and Savior, Jesus Christ" (2 Peter 1:1). The same belief is found repeatedly in the New Testament from the mouths of such apostles as Thomas (John 20:28), Paul (Rom. 9:5; Titus 2:13), and John (John 1:1, 18; Rev. 1:8; 21:6; 22:13). Following the period of the apostles, the church fathers continued to echo the same belief, as did the creeds and later confessions of the church to the present day.

But what about Jesus? Did people simply ascribe to Him this status alongside God the Father, so that He was truly also this God of Israel and the world, or did Jesus also declare Himself to be God? There are a number of passages of New Testament Scripture that demonstrate that Jesus identified Himself as being equally the same God as the Father, and also that He declared Himself to be God.

One passage shows the violent reaction of the people. When Jesus told the crowds that Abraham had looked to His day and was glad, the people retorted that Jesus was less than fifty years of age (John 8:57), so how could He have had familiarity with Abraham. Jesus replied, "Before Abraham was born, I AM" (John 8:58). At these words the people took up stones to stone Him because it was obvious that Jesus identified Himself with Yahweh, God of Israel. Moses encountered the delivering God on Mt. Sinai, in which God said that He was the I AM (Exod. 3:14), and now Jesus makes the same statement. There is no confusion in the minds of the people regarding His claim and their natural response was to stone Him for blasphemy (John 8:59).

In John 10:30, Jesus declares that He and the Father are one. One must carefully read this text since it might appear to imply nothing more than a common purpose of Jesus and the Father. More literally the text reads, "I and the Father, we are one thing." Such a declaration was viewed as blasphemous, to declare oneself and the Father as being the same. Yet here we have an important distinction and an identification of His person and being. The Father and Son are distinct persons, but they share the exact same being. The response of the crowds, as in John 8, is expected and reasonable, if Jesus was not who He claimed to be. Note the drama: "The Jews picked up stones again to stone Him. Jesus answered them, 'I showed you many good works from the Father; for which of them are you stoning Me?' The Jews answered Him, 'For a good work we do not stone You, but for blasphemy; and because You, being a man, make Yourself out to be God'" (John 10:31–33). Jesus was clear in His teaching and they understood this teaching properly.

In a similar vein Jesus proclaims Himself to be on a par with God the Father in their work, something no normal person, especially a Jew, would ever declare: "My Father is working until now, and I Myself am working" (John 5:17). This is no small claim from an observant Jew, as was Jesus, and as before, the crowds sought to kill Him for His claim: "For this reason therefore the Jews were seeking all the more to kill Him, because He not only was breaking the Sabbath, but also was calling God His own Father, making Himself equal with God" (John 5:18).

Not only did the words from the mouth of Jesus set forth His deity; so did His works. When He stilled the storm on the lake of Galilee, the response of the apostles was quite different from the crowds who wanted to stone Jesus. His disciples exclaim, "You are certainly God's Son!" (Matt. 14:33). Spiritual beings also were well aware of who the Lord of the universe was, and when they encountered Jesus they knew His power to cast them out and made proper obeisance: "Whenever the unclean spirits saw Him, they would fall down before Him and shout, 'You are the Son of God!'" (Mark 3:11). Another time Jesus forgave a paralytic man of his sins, which pronouncement brought immediate recrimination from those hearing Him: "And Jesus seeing their faith said to the paralytic, 'Son, your sins are forgiven.' But some of the scribes were sitting there and reasoning in their hearts, 'Why does this man speak that way? He is blaspheming; who can forgive sins but God alone?'" (Mark 2:5–7). The scribes who responded were not wrong in their assessment; only God can forgive sins. What they were wrong about was that they did not acknowledge that the person who stood before them was not only man, whom they could see with their eyes, but God, whom they did not see with the eyes of faith. Since the forgiveness of sins could not be viewed with the physical eyes, Jesus also healed the man of his sickness, and then declared: "Which is easier, to say to the paralytic, 'Your sins are forgiven'; or to say, 'Get up, and pick up your pallet and walk'? But so that you may know that the Son of Man has authority on earth to forgive sins"—He said to the paralytic, 'I say to you, get up, pick up your pallet and go home'" (Mark 2:9–11).

Only one other proof that He was indeed God was offered from the mouth of Jesus to the people, and that is His words when He stood before the high priest at His trial in the Sanhedrin. The high priest insisted that Jesus clearly acknowledge whether He viewed Himself as the Son of God. Note the words in Matthew's gospel when the high priest asked about the title, Son of God. Jesus responds with His self-designation (based on Dan 7:13–14) of Son of Man: "And the high priest said to Him, 'I adjure You by the living God, that You tell us whether You are the Christ, the Son of God.' Jesus said to him, 'You have said it *yourself;* nevertheless I tell you, hereafter you will see THE SON OF MAN SITTING AT THE RIGHT HAND OF POWER, and COMING ON THE CLOUDS OF HEAVEN'" (Matt. 26:63–64; see the parallel in Luke 22:69–71). The self-designation of Jesus as the Son of Man settled the issue for the high priest and for the remainder of the Sanhedrin. To declare oneself Son of Man, which was a divine title that only occurs in the mouth of Jesus in the New Testament, hearkens back to the Son of Man in Daniel 7:13–14, well known to His hearers. They did not miss the reference and viewed His words as blasphemous. Nor did they miss the impact of His statement. They were judging Him, but He was telling them that He would one day be returning from heaven in judgment of them.

Among much other evidence that could be adduced, let us look at the words of Jesus in the last book of the Bible. John presents the almighty God as the Alpha and Omega, who is the I AM ("who is and who was and who is to come"; Rev. 1:8). Yet later in the book, the resurrected Jesus declares Himself to also be the Alpha and Omega, the beginning and the end, the first and the last (Rev. 21:6;

22:13). Such a claim can only be made by one who viewed Himself as the Creator God, Sovereign of the universe; and Jesus declared Himself to be this God.

14. Was Jesus a real human?

Heretical sects in Egypt, the Gnostics, denied Christ's humanity, and the Ebionites denied His deity. But the controversy regarding Jesus in the early centuries of the church was not whether Jesus was God or man, but how the two natures related to one another and how the Son's nature as God related to the other persons and to the nature of God (see question 12). Unfortunately, the question of the hypostatic union, how two natures are in one person, became a troublesome discussion within the church. Because of this, the matter of Jesus being truly and fully human must be addressed for the purity of the church's doctrine and the honor of Jesus Christ.

To deny the humanity of the Lord Jesus is to cast a tremendous doubt on to the legitimacy of His sacrificial death and to erect a significant obstacle to our salvation. In the same way that Paul argued in 1 Corinthians 15 that if Jesus did not bodily rise from the dead, our faith is vain and we are yet in our sins, so too, if Jesus was not a complete human, His death is not sufficient to save, especially if the person of the Son is not truly God. It was necessary for the absolutely holy God to enter into human existence to offer Himself as the perfect, sinless sacrifice to satisfy the affront against Him and pay for the sinfulness of humanity.

As a truly human person, Jesus knows experientially our human struggles and can truly empathize with them. If He were part human, then His intercession as the high priest and the mediator between God and man would be incomplete and ineffectual.

The biblical text provides abundant evidence that Jesus was not partially but truly human. We discover in Matthew that before Joseph and Mary had sexual relations, she was found with child through the work of the Holy Spirit (Matt. 1:18). Luke adds additional information that the one to be born would be the Son of the Most High and reign on David's throne forever (Luke 1:26–33). In reference to His humanity, then, Jesus was a Jewish boy, in the line of Abraham and David (Matt. 1:1–17), and like all Jewish male children, He was circumcised on the eighth day as required by the law of Moses (Luke 2:22–24). Also like other Jewish boys, He went to the feasts (Luke 2:41–42) and kept the Sabbath observance (Mark 1:21; Luke 6:6), as He would for the remainder of His earthly life (Matt. 26:18; John 2:13; 7:2; 10:22–23), even though He disagreed with some of the rabbinic tradition.

Though the Son of God was fully God, the person, in His humanity, had limitations. He became hungry at times (Matt. 4:2; Mark 2:15–16) and also became tired and needed rest (John 4:6). At times He did not have knowledge of something (Mark 13:32). As well, He had human emotions such as compassion and anger and sadness (Matt. 8:10; 9:36; Luke 19:41; John 2:13–17; 11:33–35; 12:27).

Additionally, as a man, but not as God, Jesus was mortal, suffering greatly and dying on a cross (John 19:1; Luke 23:33; John 19:18). This death was not an end to the person Jesus any more than our death will end our existence as persons, nor was the death of Jesus, the end of Jesus as God. Instead, the human body was separated in death, as ours will be, from the human spirit and person. The resurrection of His body that followed afterward reunited these human elements in a powerful and incorruptible body, the model for our resurrected bodies (Luke 24:1–3, 36–43). Jesus was indeed a real human.

15. Was Jesus really born of a virgin?

The virgin birth of Jesus has been central to the church's beliefs regarding Jesus from the earliest periods. It is based on specific biblical texts found in the book of Isaiah and Matthew, but it is also required by the high Christology of Christian orthodoxy. Jesus is God and man, so that were Jesus to have been born through normal sexual relations between Mary and Joseph, the teaching of the coming of God into human existence would be in peril. It is because of this centrality that the virgin birth has been defended. That is also the reason that skeptics of the Christian faith have been intent on discrediting this teaching and maligning the moral character of Mary and, by result, the integrity of the person of Christ.

The prophet Isaiah prophesied in the eighth century before Christ that a child would be born of a virgin. This prophecy is in response to the unwillingness of Ahaz to ask of Yahweh a spectacular sign as high as the heavens or deep as Sheol. Since Ahaz was unwilling to ask, Yahweh said that He would then provide a sign, namely, that a virgin would give birth, certainly not a normal happening. In fact, this fits the type of sign that Yahweh has requested. Look at the words of the prophet:

> "Then the LORD spoke again to Ahaz, saying, 'Ask a sign for yourself from the LORD your God; make it deep as Sheol or high as heaven.' But Ahaz said, 'I will not ask, nor will I test the LORD!' Then he said, 'Listen now, O house of David! Is it too slight a thing for you to try the patience of men, that you will try the patience of my God as well? Therefore the Lord Himself will give you a sign: Behold, a virgin will be with child and bear a son, and she will call His name Immanuel.'" (Isa. 7:10–14)

Some have expressed doubts about the virgin birth being taught in the Isaiah passage. They maintain that the Hebrew term *betula*, which always means "virgin," is not used in Isaiah 7:10–14. Unfortunately for this view, this alleged technical word for *virgin* is found in a passage speaking of a widow (Joel 1:8), and has a qualification "no man had had relations with her" in Genesis 24:16. In Canaanite literature (Ugaritic), the term is used of the goddess Anath, who was hardly a virgin.[1] On the other hand, *almah*, rather than meaning merely young woman, in several places in the Old Testament clearly refers to a virgin (Song of Songs 1:3; 6:8; Gen.

24:43; Exod. 2:8; Prov. 30:19). Rather than continue argument on the uses of these terms, suffice it to say that the Greek Old Testament translators use the Greek word *parthenos*, a technical term for one who has not had sexual intercourse, as a translation of the Hebrew word *almah* (Matt. 1:22–23).[2]

More importantly, the apostle Matthew, in his gospel, considered this text from Isaiah to be literally fulfilled in the conception and birth of Jesus the Messiah. He quotes the text of Isaiah 7:14 representing the Greek Old Testament and, lest there be any misunderstanding, Matthew (1:24–25) adds, "And Joseph awoke from his sleep and did as the angel of the Lord commanded him, and took Mary as his wife, but *kept her a virgin until* she gave birth to a Son; and he called His name Jesus" (italics added).

The gospel of Luke also confirms the virgin birth in Luke 3:23, where one notices the statement regarding Jesus in the following genealogy, namely, "Jesus . . . as was supposed, the son of Joseph" (Luke 3:23). According to the Greek grammar of the passage, this statement "as was supposed" can only go with Joseph and not the comment "about thirty years."

Finally, Jesus could not have been born physically of the line of Joseph since there was a curse on that line in the Old Testament, but He could be born in the line of Mary, from Nathan, which He was, qualifying Him as a physical son of David through Mary, and a legal son of David through Joseph. This was necessary since a curse from Yahweh was placed on the line of Jeconiah (Coniah) that no son from Solomon's line through him would sit on David's throne (Jer. 22:30). Had Jesus been through Joseph's line, He would have been disqualified.

16. Did Jesus cease to be God in any respect upon becoming a man?

The orthodox teaching regarding Jesus has affirmed that Jesus was fully God and fully man. This includes the entirety of His earthly life and continues forever. Many have intended to confess this important teaching of the church but, in trying to reconcile the divine and human attributes and works of Christ, have adopted what is known as the Kenotic heresy. Essentially what the view advocates is that some essential aspect of the divine nature is lost or limited in the Son when He took upon Himself humanity. The reason for this perspective relates to the term *ekenosin*, meaning "to empty." Jesus, under the theory, is said to empty Himself of something when He became a man. Just what He emptied Himself of has been explained in the following ways, with each being less offensive to orthodoxy as they descend:

1. He emptied Himself of His *divine consciousness*, laying aside His Godhead to become a man.
2. He emptied Himself of the *eternity form of being*, exchanging His eternal form of God, for a time bound to human nature and unable to exercise divine attributes.
3. He emptied Himself of the *relative attributes of deity*, such as omnipotence and omniscience, but retained other attributes such as truth, holiness, and love.
4. He emptied Himself of the *integrity of infinite divine existence*, in which He was unaware of the attributes of the divine nature, living a double life.
5. He emptied Himself of *divine activity*, surrendering all of the divine roles and duties to the Father, so that He did not know or experience the activity of the being of God.
6. He emptied Himself of the *actual exercise of divine prerogatives*, having only the potentiality of the divine attributes but not the actual access.

There are also two sub-Kenotic theories that some have held that also fall short of the biblical teaching:

1. He emptied Himself of the *use of the divine attributes*, possessing the divine attributes but choosing not to exercise them.

2. He emptied Himself of the *independent exercise of the divine attributes*, so that the Son always possessed the attributes of God and exercised them, but always in reliance on the Father and the Spirit, never by virtue of His own deity.

Each of the above theories accepts in some measure that something of God is lost when Jesus became a human, though the manner in which this is so becomes more egregious as one moves from the first view downward.

A major passage that concerns this issue is Philippians 2:5–8, which reads: "Make your own attitude that of Christ Jesus, who, existing in the form of God, did not consider equality with God as something to be used for His own advantage. Instead He emptied Himself by assuming the form of a slave, taking on the likeness of men. And when He had come as a man in His external form, He humbled Himself by becoming obedient to the point of death—even to death on a cross" (Phil 2:5–8 HCSB). In this passage the apostle is trying to encourage his hearers to develop an attitude of humility by having them imitate Jesus. The Lord was in a far superior position than were Paul's hearers and yet He became humble; surely, Christians should have humility in view of their low estate by comparison.

In order to prove his point, the apostle mentions that Jesus existed in the very "form" of God, the Greek word speaking of having the very nature and essence of deity. One cannot be part God in Christian theology. For example, God cannot be partially omniscient or omnipresent or an infinite God who is also finite. God's attributes, shared in their entirety by the three persons, must be eternal, actual, and active. This being the case, Jesus could not cease being God and acting as God. Though He was God in every respect and equal as a person with all members of the Trinity, He emptied Himself. Note that we did not say emptied Himself of something, only that He emptied Himself. This is merely a term used to express the movement of the divine person into humanity. In fact, *emptied* is a verb and what follows is a participle in Greek explaining how the emptying occurs. He emptied Himself by taking the form of a slave, by taking the likeness of man.

When the person Jesus acted as a human on earth with all of these limitations, the same person was simultaneously acting as God on the earth and in heaven. He said while in His earthly existence, "My Father is working until now, and I Myself am working" (John 5:17), performing divine works while still a man. He said, the Son of Man has power on earth to forgive sins (Luke 5:24), something that only God could do. When He stilled the waters and the storm on the lake of Galilee (Mark 4:39), He acted as the God of creation using human instrumentality. Finally, before His death, He said, "I lay down My life so that I may take it again" (John 10:17). By His divine power as God, He controlled His own death and resurrection, raising Himself. Yet we also understand that the Father was involved in the resurrection as God, as was the Spirit, but this in no way diminishes that He was using His *own* divine prerogative to perform the act. In summary, Jesus is fully God and fully man, working through each nature with integrity, operating in each nature consistent with the capacity of each nature.

17. In what sense did Jesus understand the term *Son of Man*?

The term *Son of Man* is used eighty-eight times in the New Testament and is only used by Jesus when speaking of Himself. Though this phrase is used 107 times in the Old Testament, the way in which Jesus uses the term relates to the reference in Daniel 7:13, where one "like a Son of Man" comes before God, who is called "the Ancient of Days." The description of the Son of Man indicates a person far greater than an ordinary human; this one has divine qualities and stands in the very presence of God. To the Son of Man was given an eternal kingdom, glory, and dominion (Dan. 7:13–14). Such rule is similar to what one observes in Isaiah 9:6–7, in which the child who is born is also a son who is given the throne of King David and royal honor. This parallels the manner in which Jesus is portrayed in the New Testament. To this amazing, divine person is given an eternal kingdom that stems from the Davidic lineage.

The usage of Son of Man in the New Testament, then, reflects this idea of Son, particularly the Daniel text, more than other usages in the Old Testament. When Jesus heals a paralytic and sees his faith, Jesus declares the man's sins forgiven (Matt. 9:2). To those listening, Jesus has proclaimed blasphemy, but the Lord responds: "'But so that you may know that the Son of Man has authority on earth to forgive sins'—then He said to the paralytic, 'Get up, pick up your bed and go home'" (Matt. 9:6). On another occasion Jesus calls Himself Son of Man and He asserts that as Son of Man, He has life in Himself (John 5:26), and that He has been given authority to judge because He is the Son of Man (John 5:27). Numerous other examples could be given, but we will examine only one more, perhaps the most significant one since Jesus' self-identification as Son of Man before the Sanhedrin condemned Him to death.

Caiaphas, the high priest, tries to get Jesus to respond to the charges of false witnesses, and Jesus does not; then he asks Jesus directly, "Are You the Christ, the Son of the Blessed One [euphemism for God]?" to which Jesus replies, "I am." But He followed this confession with the words "and you shall see THE SON OF MAN SEATED AT THE RIGHT HAND OF POWER, and COMING WITH THE CLOUDS OF HEAVEN" (Mark 14:62). Admitting to be the Messiah would not in itself bring a charge of blasphemy, but the additional claim to be the Son of Man did. Claiming the kind of association with God that was understood to be true of the Daniel title *Son of Man* was blasphemy. The additional words of Jesus make it plain that this was the connection that He and the Sanhedrin both understood: "and you shall see THE SON OF MAN SEATED AT THE RIGHT HAND OF POWER and COMING WITH THE CLOUDS OF HEAVEN" (Mark 14:62). There could be no mistake. Jesus claimed identification with the Son of Man in Daniel 7:13, a divine figure who would, in fact, judge all of these who were presumptuous enough to attempt to judge Him.

18. What are the biblical designations for Jesus?

The name Yeshua', from which we have derived Jesus, was a very popular name in the first century A.D. and it is the primary designation that we have to speak of the second person of the Trinity, whether we are speaking of the deity or humanity. Yet, Jesus has several names by which He may be called. The difference in the names sometimes relates to whether we are speaking of the Son of God in reference to His divine nature and workings or His human nature. There are far too many names to set forth in a short study, and even too much that could be written of those that we do present. Let us look at some of the more well-known and often most important names of our God and Savior, Jesus the Messiah.

Jesus is known as the *Son of God*. This pertains to His eternal status and relationship with the Father from all eternity. He has always been Son of the Father before time began. The person who is the Son of God then added human nature to His person but continued as Son of God.

Jesus is also *Son of Man*, but this designation does not refer to His being just a human being. Rather, this designation is used only by Jesus in the New Testament when He is referring to Himself. It refers back to Daniel 7:13, speaking of the individual who comes before the Ancient of Days and is given an eternal kingdom of rule. That Jesus uses the phrase in this manner may be seen in two ways. First, this was a characteristic understanding of Messiah in literature of the intertestamental period and was adopted by Jesus. Second, His use of the phrase in the Gospels reveals that it was a name for sovereign God (Matt. 9:6; 10:23; 12:8; 13:41; 16:13, 28; 17:9, 12; 19:28; 20:18, 28; 24:27, 30, 37, 39, 44; 25:31; 26:2, 24, 64; Mark 2:10, 28; 8:31, 38; 14:62).

Logos is a Greek word that means "word, thought, statement, expression" and refers to Jesus being the revelation of God. The one who faced the Father and has been with the Father for eternity was also God (John 1:1), and He perfectly reveals the Father (John 1:18; 14:9).

Jesus is called *Messiah*, meaning "anointed one." He is the one prophesied in the Old Testament who, as the Son of David (Isa. 11:1–2; Jer. 23:5–6), would set up the kingdom of God on earth and reign over the people of God (Isa. 9:7). He is also the suffering servant of Yahweh (Isa. 52:13–53:12), who would take the judgment of God upon Himself and deliver His people.

Savior is one of the most magnificent names of Jesus because we personally know Him in this manner as "our" Savior. The angel told Mary that He would save His people from their sins, and John says in 3:16 that the Father sent His Son to save from their sins all who would believe in Him. Both Paul and Peter speak of Jesus and "our God and Savior," bringing together the divine and human aspects of the person Jesus, as well as His nature and work (Titus 2:13; 2 Peter 1:1).

When Jesus is called *Lord*, we may understand this to be a title of respect in some instances, but at other times it is clearly a reference to His divine person (John 20:28; Phil. 2:11). This use of Lord reflects the Greek Old Testament's use of *kurios* for the Hebrew *Yahweh*, the personal name of God in the Old Testament.

19. What was Jesus' view of the Pharisees, and did He agree with their theology?

When one thinks of a Pharisee, there is generally a negative perspective that comes to mind. A Pharisee, ostensibly, is legalistic, sour, vicious, judgmental, and the like. Much of this attitude toward these historical figures relates to the words of Jesus that one reads in the New Testament. Is this a proper portrayal of these first-century Jews with whom Jesus had much contact? The question that we are posing is not "Was Jesus a Pharisee?" but "Did He agree with the Pharisees in their theology?" Though there is certainly credible evidence in the Gospels and history that certain Pharisees were like the Pharisee mentioned above, is it fair to paint such a broad picture of them? Moreover, even if certain or most Pharisees satisfy this description in their daily lives, does this mean that their teaching was not true regarding important areas of theology?

We must be careful in how we understand the words of the Gospel texts as they speak of the Pharisees, or for that matter, the Jews. Some of the words of Jesus against the Jews have been viewed wrongly as anti-Semitic because of their harshness, but this can hardly be the intent of the text, since the Gospel writers, Jesus, and His hearers were primarily Jews. When the expression "the Jews," and probably "the Pharisees," is used accusatorially, it speaks not of all Jews or all Pharisees but of the specific ones within the larger group who opposed Jesus or failed to be consistent with their profession. He called them a "brood of vipers" (Matt. 12:34) and rebuked them for pompous prayer (Luke 18:10–14).

Jesus used scolding remarks, as did John the Baptist (Matt. 3:7), against insincere Pharisees and scholars who came to Him, but there are other Pharisees who had a true heart of belief or, at least, were not within the class He criticized. For example, Nicodemus and Joseph of Arimathea (who was probably a Pharisee) embraced Christ. On another occasion, Jesus was invited to eat a meal with a Pharisee (Luke 7:36), an invitation He accepted. We also see Pharisees supporting Jesus (Mark 12:28; Luke 13:31), and John 9:16 indicates a division among the Pharisees about the works of Jesus and His character, so it is clear that not all opposed Him. Jesus said that the Pharisees sat on Moses' seat (Matt. 23:2) and were to be believed in their teaching, though not when they acted hypocritically. Interestingly, we find in the Jewish writings stinging criticism of the Pharisees within their own ranks. New Testament scholar Bruce Metzger summarizes the Talmud's list of seven types of Pharisees, in which it vividly ridicules five of them:

1. The "wait-a-little" Pharisee always has an excuse for putting off doing a good deed.
2. The "bruised" or "bleeding" Pharisee, in order to avoid looking at a woman, shuts his eyes and stumbles against the wall so as to bruise himself and bleed.

3. The "shoulder" Pharisee wears, as it were, his good deeds ostentatiously upon his shoulders, where all can see them.
4. The "hump-backed" Pharisee walks about stooped over in mock humility.
5. The "ever-reckoning" Pharisee is continually counting up his good deeds to balance them against his bad deeds.
6. The "God-fearing" Pharisee stands in awe and dread of God.
7. The "God-loving" or "born" Pharisee is a true son of Abraham and a genuine Pharisee.[3]

After the time of Christ, we also observe the Pharisees in a favorable light at times. We find at one instance that Gamaliel, a leader among the Pharisees, protected the disciples by urging toleration before the Sanhedrin (Acts 5:33–39). The Pharisees sided with Paul against the Sadducees (Acts 23:6–9), and a group of Pharisees were even called believers (Acts 15:5). More importantly, Paul proudly identifies himself as a Pharisee (Acts 23:6; Phil. 3:5–6).

In spite of the fact that Jesus disagreed with many Pharisees about the understanding of the oral law and rebuked their practice of the law, He nonetheless found considerable agreement with the theology of the Pharisees. Note the similarities:

- The Pharisees believed in the resurrection of the body and the immortality of the soul (Matt. 22:23–32).
- The Pharisees believed in angels and demons (Matt. 9:34; Acts 23:8).
- The Pharisees held to a doctrine of foreordination and viewed this as consistent with the free will of humans (Josephus, *Antiquities* 13.5.9; 18.1.3).
- The Pharisees believed in a coming judgment and in a future punishment and reception of rewards according to whether one had lived virtuously or not (Acts 23:8).
- The Pharisees believed in an all-wise and knowledgeable God, who was both just and merciful (Luke 5:21).[4]

Certainly some have attempted to demonstrate that Jesus was a Pharisee. This is because the people of Israel were divided into different religious and political groups and views such as the Herodians, Sadducees, Zealots, Pharisees, and Essenes. Consequently, the argument goes that even if Jesus did not officially belong to a local Pharisee group, He would be a Pharisee by view and disposition. Since the Pharisees were the "party of the people," this would be the most likely one to follow. Secondly, though Jesus said many negative things against Pharisees, He also says that the Pharisees sat on Moses' seat (Matt. 23:2) so people should believe their teachings, but they should not follow the hypocrisy of the Pharisees (Matt. 23:2). However, there is no basis to argue that Jesus was part of any party of the Pharisees. He came with a superior message to theirs, and He came with a morally perfect life. He came to begin His own community and build the kingdom of God, not to advocate Pharisaic ideas or reform the movement.

20. What was the transfiguration of Jesus and why did it happen?

Toward the end of Jesus' life, He took His inner circle of disciples—Peter, James, and John—to a high mountain, to reveal Himself to them in a manner He had not done so before (Matt. 17:1–8; Mark 9:1–8). Some have identified this event as having occurred on Mt. Tabor in Galilee, but this mountain is one among many others nearby, so it does not seem to be accurately designated as a high mountain. The transfiguration probably occurred on Mt. Hermon, in the southern area of Lebanon, a mountain of several thousand feet, which also fits geographically with His ministry in the northern portion of Israel.

At the beginning of Jesus' ministry, at His baptism, the Father's voice came from heaven, and the Spirit of God manifested Himself in the form of a dove to identify Jesus as the chosen one, the Messiah promised in the Old Testament. The transfiguration also has the voice of the Father echoing over the disciples that Jesus was the beloved Son of the Father. There are several points of distinction between these two events, however, and these differences have important theological emphases.

In the baptism Jesus appeared as any other man, identifying Himself with the people of Israel. At the transfiguration, He is revealed as God, with the radiance of God, the Shekinah glory shining through His flesh (Matt. 17:2–3), the only Son of the Father. At this transfiguration, the apostle Peter wanted to level Jesus alongside the heroes of Israel, Moses and Elijah, who represented the Law and the Prophets, building a tabernacle for each of them. Though these great prophets had an important place in the history of Israel and salvation, Jesus stands by Himself as the complete and final revelation of God and as the Savior of mankind; consequently, the Father has these prophets disappear, leaving only Jesus with the disciples, with the admonition to listen to Him (Matt. 17:5–8).

PART 3

The Work of Jesus According to the Bible

21. How did Jesus fulfill Old Testament prophecies?

Those who believe that the Hebrew Scriptures contain predictions regarding a future Messiah who would establish a kingdom of God on the earth and give Himself as a sacrifice for the sins of humanity must still answer the question, was Jesus *this* Messiah?[1] There have been thousands of persons, from the time of Jesus until the present, claiming to be or proclaimed by others to be the promised "anointed one" of God spoken of in the Old Testament.[2]

In order for Jesus to have been the Messiah spoken about in the Hebrew Bible, it is necessary that He fulfill the myriad of prophecies of the Old Testament. Various Messiahs came forth in the days of Jesus and since, but their lives, words, and actions did not satisfy the biblical predictions about Messiah.[3] Jesus declared that He did fulfill the qualifications of the promised "anointed one" (Messiah). Toward the beginning of His ministry, when speaking at His home synagogue in Nazareth, He was given the scroll of Isaiah to read before the congregants. It "just so happened" that the reading that day was from Isaiah 61. Verses 1 and 2 read, "The Spirit of the LORD Yahweh is on Me, because Yahweh has anointed

Me to bear good news to the weak. He has sent Me to bind the one broken of heart, to proclaim liberty to the captives, and freedom to prisoners. To proclaim the year of Yawheh's favor . . ." (personal translation). According to Luke 4:18, at this point in verse 2, Jesus of Nazareth ceased His reading and said that the words He had just read were fulfilled that day. This identification of Messiah with Himself at the synagogue caused the people in the synagogue to rise against Him and they attempted to kill Him.

What is particularly interesting about this fulfillment is that Jesus saw Himself as only fulfilling this prophecy up through Isaiah 61:2a, stopping short of reading the next half of the verse that speaks of "the day of vengeance of our God," which is something that occurs at the second coming of Jesus. After His resurrection, Jesus met two of His disciples on the road to Emmaus (Luke 24:13), but He kept them from recognizing Him (Luke 24:16), appearing only as a stranger. They spoke to Jesus as they walked, about the events that had transpired regarding their crucified master (Luke 24:19–24). Jesus replied, "How unwise and slow you are to believe in your hearts all that the prophets have spoken! Didn't the Messiah have to suffer these things and enter into His glory?" (Luke 24:25–26 HCSB). The failure to believe in Jesus as Messiah was not restricted to these two persons walking with Jesus that day but was characterized by the apostles as they hid from the authorities. Jesus then proceeded to demonstrate that the Hebrew Scriptures prophesied of Him (Luke 24:27).[4]

That Jesus spoke truthfully of being the fulfillment of the Old Testament becomes evident when we look at the way He speaks and acts in the Gospels and the manner in which the apostles speak about Him in their writings. Each of the prophecies in the New Testament regarding the Messiah is fulfilled literally and follows the same method of interpretation as used by the rabbis of the time (see question 9). Observe all of the ways in which the various Old Testament predictions were fulfilled in Jesus the Messiah as recorded in the New Testament writings:

Prediction	OT Passage	NT Fulfillment	NT Passage
Messiah would preexist before His birth.	Mic. 5:2	He is before all things. He is the creator of all things.	Col. 1:17; John 1:2 John 1:3
Messiah would be the Prophet prophesied by Moses.	Deut. 18:18	He is declared a prophet by the crowds. He is declared a prophet by the apostles.	Matt. 21:11 Acts 3:21–22
Messiah would be the fulfillment of the covenant to Abraham.	Gen. 12:1–3	Jesus the Messiah became the fulfillment of the Abrahamic covenant's promise of blessing to the Gentiles.	Acts 3:24–26; Gal. 3:6–9, 14
Messiah would be born of a virgin.	Isa. 7:14	He is born of a young virgin named Mary. He only seemed to be the son of Joseph.	Matt. 1:18, 22–23 Luke 3:23
Messiah would come from the seed of Abraham, Isaac, and Jacob.	Gen. 22:18; 21:12; Num. 24:19	The lineage recorded in Matthew and Luke indicates that He was in direct line to Abraham through Isaac and Jacob.	Matt. 1:1; Luke 3:23, 34
Messiah would be of the house of David.	Jer. 23:5	The lineage recorded in Matthew and Luke reveals that He is the Son of David.	Luke 3:23–30
Messiah would be called Immanuel.	Isa. 7:14	Matthew records the message of the angel to Joseph declaring that Jesus is Immanuel, Son of God	Matt. 1:21–23

Prediction	OT Passage	NT Fulfillment	NT Passage
Messiah would be born in Bethlehem.	Mic. 5:2	Matthew records that Jesus was born in Bethlehem of Judea	Matt. 2:1, 4
Messiah would ride into Jerusalem on a donkey.	Zech. 9:9	Jesus made a triumphal entry on a donkey (cf. Matt. 21:1–11) on Palm Sunday, almost a week before His crucifixion.	Matt. 21:1–11; Mark 11:1–11; Luke 19:29–44; John 12:12–19
Messiah would be betrayed by a friend.	Ps. 41:9	Jesus speaks of Judas as a friend at His betrayal in the garden of Gethsemane.	Matt. 26:50; John 13:18
Messiah would be rejected by His own people.	Ps. 118:22	The apostle Peter sees this Old Testament text as referring to the Messiah's rejection.	1 Peter 2:5–6
Messiah would be betrayed for thirty pieces of silver.	Zech. 11:12	Judas offered to betray the Messiah for thirty pieces of silver.	Matt. 26:14–16
Messiah's betrayer's money would be thrown into a field.	Zech. 11:13	When Judas's remorse caused him to approach the chief priests with an offer to return the money, they used it to buy a potter's field.	Matt. 27:4–8
The seed of woman would crush the head of Satan.	Gen. 3:15	The Messiah fulfills this prediction in Genesis 3, the Son of God, coming as a man and bringing judgment on Satan at the cross.	Col. 2:14–15

Prediction	OT Passage	NT Fulfillment	NT Passage
Messiah would be crucified.	Isa. 53:5, 12	The apostles record that Jesus the Messiah was crucified by the Romans.	Matt. 27:22, 23, 34–50; Mark 15:14–33; Luke 23:22, 32–33; John 19:15–42; Acts 2:35–36; 4:10; 1 Cor. 1; 2:1, 7
Messiah would be pierced in His side.	Isa. 53:5; Zech. 12:10	The Roman soldiers pierced His side to verify that He had died.	John 19:34, 37
Messiah would not have any bones broken.	Exod. 12:46	Jesus died before the Roman soldiers broke His bones, as they did with those crucified with Him.	John 19:33, 36
Messiah would be buried in a rich man's tomb.	Isa. 53:9	Jesus was buried in the newly cutout tomb of a rich man named Joseph.	Matt. 27:57–61
Messiah would be resurrected from the dead.	Ps. 16:10	In agreement with Scripture, Jesus the Messiah rose from the dead.	Acts 2:29–32; 1 Cor. 15:3–11

A review of these and other prophecies with their fulfillments demonstrates that Jesus of Nazareth, who was crucified and rose again, is the true Messiah spoken about in the prophets of the Old Testament. Even as the prophecies of the Hebrew Scriptures foretold His coming as a baby in Bethlehem, born to die for the sins of humanity (Matt. 1:21; John 3:16), so, too, along with New Testament prophecies, He will come again in literal fashion (1 Thess. 4:14; 1 John 3:2) to take His people to be with Him and judge humanity (Acts 17:31) for their rejection of God's call.

22. In what way was Jesus a prophet?

Yahweh spoke to Israel in the fifteenth century B.C., promising to raise up a prophet from among Israel, in whose mouth He would place His words. This prophet would faithfully speak for Yahweh, and all those who fail to heed these words would be held accountable (Deut. 18:15–19).

Generally conservative Christian scholars would identify the Deuteronomy 18 prophet as Jesus the Messiah. The response of the general populace (those who heard Him gladly, Mark 12:37 KJV) was that they believed Jesus to be a prophet (Matt. 21:11; Luke 7:16; John 4:19). Some seem to have identified Jesus with the unique prophet promised in the Old Testament (John 6:14; 7:40). This is further substantiated by the words of the apostle Peter, who identifies Jesus specifically with Deuteronomy 18 as he writes, "'and that He may send Jesus, the Christ appointed for you, whom heaven must receive until the period of restoration of all things about which God spoke by the mouth of His holy prophets from ancient time. Moses said, 'THE LORD GOD WILL RAISE UP FOR YOU A PROPHET LIKE ME FROM YOUR BRETHREN; TO HIM YOU SHALL GIVE HEED to everything He says to you. And it will be that every soul that does not heed that prophet shall be utterly destroyed from among the people'" (Acts 3:20–23).

Jesus the Messiah is not only recognized by the people and apostles as being a prophet, but His words and works show this to be true. The manner in which He spoke the Word of God, as prophets of old had done, connects Him to them. He foretold the future about the coming destruction of the city of Jerusalem (Matt. 24:1–2) and the temple, something that was not believed by the Jews until the very end in A.D. 70. At the time of the coming of the Babylonians (Jer. 7), many of the Jewish leaders believed that God's city and house must always stand; in the days of Jesus, there was the same sentiment. The Jewish leadership that rebelled against the Romans trusted in the temple to rescue them from the Romans after they had abandoned the true God and killed His

Son (Matt. 21:32–35, 37–43). Jesus also functioned prophetically in denouncing the sins of the leaders and the people and called them to repentance, even as Jeremiah did, in the midst of the temple grounds (Matt. 21:12–13; Mark 11:15–18). In a scathing rebuke of the Jewish leaders and with the fervor of the Old Testament prophets, He called them to repent, mend their ways, and turn to God if they were to escape God's judgment (Matt. 23). Even as the Hebrew prophets before Him, He also did miracles in the sight of the people, but in far greater number and power than did any other prophet. He healed the lame and blind, the palsy and those inflicted with leprosy, and raised the dead in a manner that no one had ever done, after several days in the tomb. This is because He was also more than a prophet. He was God in the flesh, the resurrection and the life (John 11:25–27).

23. In what way was Jesus a priest?

That Jesus was a priest is clearly shown in the New Testament. He offered a sacrifice acceptable to God for the sins of the people, but in a way that was superior to all other sacrifices that had ever been offered before, by offering Himself. He did not satisfy the requirement of being part of the Aaronic priesthood, but He was a greater priest as Psalm 110:4 speaks of Messiah, a priest like Melchizedek. The writer of Hebrews develops this idea in great depth, and calls Jesus "the Apostle and High Priest of our confession" (Heb. 3:1). As the author of this magnificent book discusses the Melchizedek priesthood, he ties this unique priesthood to Jesus' position as Son. Note the words, "So also Christ did not glorify Himself so as to become a high priest, but He who said to Him, 'YOU ARE MY SON, TODAY I HAVE BEGOTTEN YOU; just as He says also in another passage, 'YOU ARE A PRIEST FOREVER ACCORDING TO THE ORDER OF MELCHIZEDEK'" (Heb. 5:5–6). Unlike the temporary priests who served in the temple offering sacrifices that did not forgive sins but merely covered them over, in anticipation of the perfect sacrifice of God to be offered, Jesus' priesthood relates not to ancestry but to

His "indestructible life" (Heb. 7:15–17). John Paul II captures succinctly this role of priest for the Christ:

> Finally, we can note that the Letter to the Hebrews states clearly and convincingly that Jesus Christ has fulfilled with his whole life, and especially with the sacrifice of the cross, all that was written in the messianic tradition of divine revelation. His priesthood is situated in reference to the ritual service of the priests of the old covenant, which he surpasses as priest and victim. God's eternal design which provides for the institution of the priesthood in the history of the covenant is fulfilled in Christ.[5]

24. In what way was Jesus a king?

In Hebrew thought, the identification of Jesus as king is directly connected to Him being Messiah (from Hebrew *māšîaḥ*, the anointed one). The kings of Israel were the anointed ones of God (1 Sam. 15:1), a type of the future king to sit on David's throne with an everlasting dominion (Isa. 9:6–7). Note the words of Jeremiah, "'Behold, the days are coming,' declares the LORD, 'When I will raise up for David a righteous Branch; And He will reign as king and act wisely And do justice and righteousness in the land'" (Jer. 23:5).

Though Jesus never called Himself a king, the prophecy that Jesus fulfilled declares Him to be a king (Zech. 9:9); the wise men adored (Matt. 2:1–2, 9–12) and Herod feared the baby born king (Matt. 2:3–4, 16–18); the crowds hailed Him as such (Matt. 21:9, 15; Mark 11:9–10; John 12:13) and His disciples considered Him to be king (John 1.49); His enemies accused Him of claiming to be king (Luke 23:2; John 19:12) and mocked Him for this perceived claim (Matt. 27:29, 37, 42), but Pilate, ironically, confirmed that He was King of the Jews (Matt. 27:37); the authors of the New Testament believed Him to be king (1 Tim. 1:16–17; Rev. 17:14; 19:15–16) and Jesus indicated before Pilate that He was king of another world (John 18:33–37), but before the Sanhedrin,

He clearly indicated that He would return as King at His second coming (Mark 14:62).

The significance of Jesus' kingship is that as the Son of David, the king, He has a right to be legal heir as king over the nation of Israel. As God, the Son has been king over the universe, but the significance of Jesus' kingship as a son of David is that He has a legal right to reign over the nation of Israel, something to occur yet in the future. At the present, He is sitting on His throne in heaven with the Father, but at His coming He will put down all opposition and sit on David's throne—His own throne—in Jerusalem (Pss. 2:6–9; 110:1–2; Matt. 25:31, 34; Col. 3:1).

25. Why did Jesus need to be baptized?

The baptism of Jesus is recorded in Matthew 3:13–17 and briefly mentioned in Mark 1:9–11 and Luke 3:21–22. The baptism is also implied and alluded to in John 1:29–34. In each of the accounts, the baptism is linked to the anointing of Jesus with the Holy Spirit and each account records God the Father's affirmation of Jesus as the Son of God, the second person of the Trinity. All three persons of the Trinity were present at the baptism. The anointing of Jesus by the Holy Spirit at His baptism was the inauguration of Jesus' three-year earthly ministry and, according to Matthew 12:18, fulfilled the prophecy of Isaiah 42:1 (see also the messianic Ps. 2:7, which identifies the Messiah as Son of God). Jesus is the Messiah-Servant. Matthew's record tells us that John the Baptist protested that he should not baptize Jesus and that the roles should be reversed—it was John who needed to repent of sin, not Jesus. Jesus acknowledged John's logic, but He insisted that John baptize Him for a different reason—"to fulfill all righteousness" (Matt. 3:15). By accepting baptism by John, Jesus validated John's message that people needed to prepare for salvation.

The anointing of Jesus with the Holy Spirit followed the pattern of the kings of Israel being anointed (1 Sam. 10:1; 1 Kings 1:34–35, 38–39; 19:16; 11:12), of priests being anointed (Exod. 28:41; 29:7;

30:30–33; 40:13–15), and of at least one prophet being anointed (1 Kings 19:16; see also 1 Chron. 16:22 and Ps. 105:15). Only in Luke's account are we told that the Holy Spirit descended while Jesus was praying during the baptism. The anointing in each of these instances marked their appointment or placement into office. Like John the Baptist, Jesus was probably filled with the Holy Spirit before birth (Luke 1:15), but the descent of the Holy Spirit on Him as a dove at the baptism visually marked Jesus as the promised Messiah and served as His induction into that biblical office. It was a visual affirmation that Jesus was the promised Messiah. It is a divine pronouncement of who Jesus is and a recognition of His ministry. He is publicly beginning that which He came to earth to do for all people. Salvation has come to people in the person of Jesus Christ, just as John had proclaimed. Three years later, the Father would again voice from heaven the same words of approval at the transfiguration of Jesus (Matt. 17:5; Mark 9:7; Luke 9:35).

26. Why did Jesus die?

The death of Jesus is the most important event in human history. It assures us of God's love for us (John 3:16; Rom. 5:8; 1 John 3:16; 4:9), and it provides a basis for our reconciliation to God (Rom. 5:11). The justice of God required that the penalty for our sins be paid, and God found a way to have that penalty paid—He sent His own Son who had no sin to pay the price by dying on the cross for our sins (2 Cor. 5:21). According to the Bible, the death of Jesus was a sacrifice for the sins of the entire world. Jesus died for the sins of all people, sins that separate us from a holy God. His death was a substitutionary death. His death was both in our place and for our benefit (2 Cor. 5:21; 1 Peter 3:18). In John 1:29, we read the words of John the Baptist, declaring, "Behold, the Lamb of God who takes away the sin of the world!" The death of Jesus was a fulfillment of Old Testament prophecies such as Isaiah 53 and many others (Luke 24:27, 44; 1 Cor. 15:3).

In addition to being a substitutionary death, the death of Christ also was a redemptive death. His death paid the price for human sin so that individuals could be redeemed. In effect, Jesus Christ through His death purchased us out of the marketplace of sin (Gal. 4:5) and it released us or liberated us. Those who believe in Jesus Christ and His death on the cross for them have the certainty that He died for them, bearing the penalty for their sins (Rom. 4:25; 2 Cor. 5:21; Gal. 1:4; Heb. 9:28). Jesus died because of the love and justice of God that compelled Him to send His Son as a substitute and sacrifice for the sins of all people.

Because of the death of Jesus, our alienation from God is eradicated when we believe in the death of Jesus Christ for our sins. His death and shed blood is the ultimate and final sacrifice that can be made for sin and it is propitiation or satisfaction to God (Rom. 3:25; 1 John 2:2); once redeemed, Christians are now free to live a life that is pleasing to God. The death of Jesus Christ is the basis for our acceptance with God. Jesus died so that each of us may have eternal life.

27. Did Jesus rise from the dead in the same body in which He died?

The Old and New Testaments record many miracles of raising the dead back to life (1 Kings 17:17–24; 2 Kings 4:17–37; Matt. 9:23–26; 10:8; Luke 7:11–15; John 11:38–44; Acts 9:36–42; 20:7–12), but these are considered to be different from the resurrection of the dead to occur at the end of this age. In the former resurrections, the people died again and await, with the rest of us, the final resurrection, either to life (John 5:28–29) or to death (Rev. 20:12–14). Prior to the resurrection of the righteous and unrighteous, those who were raised had bodies subject to decay and death, but in the future resurrection the bodies will be incorruptible and immortal.

How does all of this relate to the nature of the body of Jesus after the resurrection? We discover in Scripture that He is the firstfruits of the resurrection unto life (1 Cor. 15:20, 23). He is the first to be raised in an incorruptible and immortal body. Moreover, He was raised not in another body that He had before the resurrection, a transmigration or reincarnation, but in concert with biblical teaching, He was raised in the same physical body in which He died. The difference is that the preresurrection body had physical weakness. The body could be ill, hurt, grow weary, be hungry, but His resurrection body is raised in power. This body will never be ill nor have pain, and it will never be subject to death.

How, then, should we understand passages that speak of a spiritual body? Wasn't Jesus' resurrection, and thus believers in the future resurrection, a mixture of spirit and body, rather than distinct as we are now? No. The text is clear that He was raised in His physical body, and not in spirit-body. If the physical body is not raised, there is no resurrection. There are least three biblical texts that seem to cast doubt on the fact that Jesus was raised in the same physical body in which He died. One is the interaction with the disciples on the way to Emmaus when they did not know who He was; He ate with them and disappeared from their sight (Luke 24:13–35). Second is the failure of Mary of Magdala to recognize Jesus when she was with Him in the garden (John 20:11–18). Third, when Jesus appeared to His disciples, He appeared in the room though the door was shut (John 20:26), ostensibly because He could walk through walls in His new body.

Each of these can be easily explained when one carefully reads the context of each passage. How then, does one explain the event on the road to Emmaus, when Jesus walked with two disciples, but they didn't know who He was (Luke 24:15–16)? The text answers the quandary. It says that as they encountered Jesus "their eyes were prevented from recognizing Him" (Luke 24:16). Had their eyes not been prevented by Him, they would have quickly known who He was. Further in the passage, after He gives them thorough teaching regarding Himself in the Hebrew Scriptures, after they sat down to eat with Him, and after He took bread, broke it, and blessed it, "Then their eyes were opened and they recognized Him" (Luke 24:31). There was then no mystery, and Jesus was in the same body in which He died. He looked the same and, consequently, He kept them from knowing who He was until immediately before He disappeared from their sight (Luke 24:31).

Why did Mary fail to recognize Jesus if He appeared in the same body in which He died? Mary was in the garden early in the morning when it was still dark, and saw that the tomb was open. She reported this to Peter and John, and they all went back to the tomb, finding it empty. After the men had left, she lingered, her heart broken about the empty tomb, believing that someone had stolen the body. She saw what she thought was a gardener and inquired of this gardener regarding the body of Jesus. Note the words of John 20:14–15: "When she had said this, she turned around and saw Jesus standing there, and did not know that it was Jesus. Jesus said to her, 'Woman, why are you weeping? Whom are you seeking?' Supposing Him to be the gardener, she said to Him, 'Sir, if you have carried Him away, tell me where you have laid Him, and I will take Him away.'"

Verse 14 indicates that she did not recognize Jesus; it does not say that He was in a different body or did not look the same. Put yourself in the garden very early in the morning with the natural inability to make out a person's face before the sun rises in the sky. Add to that the fact that she was crying; obviously, she had difficulty recognizing Jesus. There was no need for Jesus to keep her from recognizing Him, as was the case when He encountered the disciples in the late afternoon on the road to Emmaus. The further statement by Jesus asking her not to touch Him (John 20:17) has caused some to think that He was not material or possibly a different substance. Such is not the case. He is imploring her to "stop clinging" (present imperative verb) to Him because He has not yet gone back to the Father (proleptic perfect). She need not be concerned, then, that He will go away immediately, so there was no need to grasp Him. We know that Jesus stayed on earth another forty days after His resurrection.

The last consideration to be explained is His sudden appearance behind closed doors at a time all of the disciples were together: "After eight days His disciples were again inside, and Thomas with them. Jesus came, the doors having been shut, and stood in their midst and said, 'Peace be with you'" (John 20:26). There is no requirement that Jesus' body be nonphysical for what we read in this passage. The text does not say that Jesus walked through a wall, implying that His body had a less-than-physical composition. Several options are available, even if not probable, such as walking unnoticed through the doorway after opening the shut (not locked) door. Or He may have simply appeared, even as He disappeared with the disciples with whom He ate in Emmaus.

Remember that what Jesus did in His resurrection body is no more spectacular than what He did in His preresurrection body, namely, walking on the water. This miracle did not require a change in the composition of His human body. The difference of the body prior to the resurrection, with Christ's body being the precursor of us all, is that it is not subject to corruption or death, not that it has nonphysical properties (1 Cor. 15:51–53). Jesus ate with the disciples by the Sea of Galilee after He made breakfast for them (John 21:12), and He ascended into the air in the ascension (Acts 1:9), but Philip also was transported after his ministry with the Ethiopian eunuch (Acts 8:39). The apostle John said that even though we don't fully understand what we shall be in the resurrection, we can be sure of this, that we will be like Him (1 John 3:2); the grandest significance of our discussion is that we will be like the Lord in His resurrection.

28. Why did Jesus send the Holy Spirit?

As Jesus' earthly ministry drew to a close and He prepared to return to heaven, He told the disciples that they would not be left alone. In John 14:16, Jesus said that He would ask God the Father to send another helper—often transliterated as *Paraclete*, literally "one called alongside." The word often had the connotation of a helper in a court of law. This helper would be the Holy Spirit, the third person of the Trinity who would be a comforter and advocate

(John 14:16–17; 15:26–27; 16:7–15). The Holy Spirit was a gift from heaven to teach the disciples and to help them remember the words and message of Jesus Christ (John 14:26). Just as Jesus was Himself an advocate, helper, and intercessor in heaven for the disciples (1 John 2:1), so too would the Holy Spirit carry on this ministry in the physical absence of Christ. In John 14:16, Jesus promises, "I will ask the Father, and He will give you another Helper, that He may be with you forever." Jesus' use of the word *another* is that of "another of the same kind." Both Jesus and the Holy Spirit are sent from God the Father into the world, both are called holy, and both are characterized by the word *truth*. In John 16:7, Jesus says that He will send the Holy Spirit. Both the Father and the Son are involved in the coming of the Holy Spirit.

In addition to serving as an advocate and in coming to the disciples and the world, the Holy Spirit would mediate the presence of God the Father and God the glorified Son (John 14:16–26) as well as serve as a teacher and revealer (John 14:26; 16:12–14). Jesus tells the disciples that when the Holy Spirit comes, He will prosecute a case against the world and will "convict the world concerning sin and righteousness and judgment" (John 16:8). The Spirit will convict or convince the world concerning sin, showing that the world is in lawlessness or opposition to God; concerning righteousness in the sense of vindication of Jesus' righteousness, which is exemplified in His return to heaven and glorification (16:10); and concerning judgment so that every person must decide, judge, or in essence "choose sides" regarding Jesus Christ (John 1:9; 8:12; see also 3:19 where John uses the same word, *krisis*, for judgment).

The Holy Spirit would have a ministry that would be unique and continue the plan of God. The Spirit's ministry would guide the disciples in the truths Jesus spoke and taught. Jesus' words in John 8:31–32, "you will know the truth, and the truth will make you free," would be fully realized under the ministry of the Holy Spirit. The Holy Spirit could not come until Jesus left (John 16:7). The coming of the Spirit was realized on the day of Pentecost (Acts

2:1–47), which inaugurated a new age in God's prophetic plan. With the coming of the Spirit, the age of the church began, and the ministry of the Holy Spirit began a new phase in God's eternal plan. The coming of the Holy Spirit advances God's plans for the world and humanity and provides a divine perpetual guide, presence, and assurance in our midst until Jesus Himself returns.

PART 4

Jesus and the Future

29. Where is Jesus now?

After His resurrection and forty days of postresurrection ministry (Acts 1:3), the disciples saw their last miracle in the presence of Jesus when He ascended to heaven on a cloud. In Acts 1:9–11, Luke states: "And after He had said these things, He was lifted up while they were looking on, and a cloud received Him out of their sight. And as they were gazing intently into the sky while He was going, behold, two men in white clothing stood beside them. They also said, 'Men of Galilee, why do you stand looking into the sky? This Jesus, who has been taken up from you into heaven, will come in just the same way as you have watched Him go into heaven.'" Also, in his gospel, Luke writes, "And He led them out as far as Bethany, and He lifted up His hands and blessed them. While He was blessing them, He parted from them and was carried up into heaven" (Luke 24:50–51).

Jesus clearly went to a place. He didn't vanish but, rather, gradually ascended into heaven after which angels told the disciples that He would one day return *in the same way.* Jesus is in a place hidden to our eyes, but still a very real place. When Stephen was dying after being stoned as recorded in Acts 7:55–56, God gave him the unique ability and comfort through the Holy Spirit to see into heaven and see Jesus Christ: "But being full of the Holy Spirit, he gazed intently into heaven and saw the glory of God, and Jesus standing at the right hand of God; and he said, 'Behold, I see the heavens opened up and the Son of Man standing at the right hand of God.'" Although we don't see heaven or fully comprehend it, it is where Jesus is now. It is a place (John 14:1–2) and upon His arrival in heaven, Jesus received glory and honor that He had not had on earth during His incarnation (John 17:5). Luke, recording Peter's sermon on the day of Pentecost, writes of this exaltation: "Therefore having been exalted to the right hand of God, and having received from the Father the promise of the Holy Spirit, He has poured forth this which you both see and hear" (Acts 2:33).

The Bible tells us that Jesus is seated at the right hand of God, fulfilling Old Testament prophecies such as Psalm 110:1, signifying the completion of His redemptive work on earth (Heb. 1:3), and receiving power and authority over the universe (1 Peter 3:22). Yet, Jesus is not perpetually seated or inactive, for we are told in Stephen's vision that Jesus is standing (Acts 7:56). In John's vision, Jesus is walking among the seven lampstands of Revelation 2:1. Many other passages also affirm Christ's present work in heaven, including: Romans 8:34; Ephesians 1:20–22; Philippians 2:6–11; 3:20; Hebrews 4:14; 6:20; 7:26; Revelation 14:1–5 and 19:11–16.[1] The ascension of Jesus is an assurance to Christians that we, too, will be with Him one day, beginning either when we are taken in death (2 Cor. 5:8) or when He returns, and then continuing into the age to come (Rev. 3:21).

30. Will Jesus really return?

Belief in the physical return of Jesus Christ is the historic and biblical position of Christianity throughout the centuries. It has been the hope and prayer of millions of Christians since the ascension of Jesus recorded in Acts 1:6–11. "He will come again to judge the living and the dead" (cf. 2 Tim. 4:1 and 1 Peter 4:5). For centuries, faithful Christians around the globe have pronounced these words and proclaimed this truth from the Apostles' Creed and a score of other creeds of Christian orthodoxy. The second coming

of Jesus Christ is the subject of many passages in both the Old
Testament and the New Testament, including: Deuteronomy 30:3;
Psalm 2; Isaiah 63:1–6; Daniel 2:44–45; 7:13–14; Zechariah 14:1–
4; Matthew 24–25; Mark 13; Luke 21; Acts 1:9–11; Romans 11:26;
1 Thessalonians 3:13; 5:1–4; 2 Thessalonians 1:6–2:12; 2 Peter 2:1–
3:17; Jude 14–15; and Revelation 1:7; 19:11–21.

There are many passages throughout the Old Testament that
describe the second coming and events surrounding it. From these
passages we learn of the reign of Christ upon the throne of David,
the government and conditions of the millennial kingdom that follow the second coming, and the judgment Christ will bring when
He returns.

As we turn to the pages of the New Testament, we find additional information. Jesus taught much about the second coming.
One vivid description occurred in response to questions the disciples asked about the event:

> For just as the lightning comes from the east and flashes
> even to the west, so will the coming of the Son of Man be.
> Wherever the corpse is, there the vultures will gather. But
> immediately after the tribulation of those days THE SUN
> WILL BE DARKENED, AND THE MOON WILL NOT GIVE ITS
> LIGHT, AND THE STARS WILL FALL from the sky, and the
> powers of the heavens will be shaken. And then the sign
> of the Son of Man will appear in the sky, and then all the
> tribes of the earth will mourn, and they will SEE THE SON
> OF MAN COMING ON THE CLOUDS OF THE SKY with power
> and great glory. (Matt. 24:27–30)

Probably the most graphic portrayal of Christ's second coming is
found in Revelation 19:11–21. In this extended passage, Jesus Christ
is described as leading a procession of angels and saints or armies
in heaven to claim the earth, destroy the armies of the world, and
defeat the Antichrist and False Prophet:

And I saw heaven opened, and behold, a white horse, and He who sat on it is called Faithful and True, and in righteousness He judges and wages war. His eyes are a flame of fire, and on His head are many diadems; and He has a name written on Him which no one knows except Himself. He is clothed with a robe dipped in blood; and His name is called The Word of God. And the armies which are in heaven, clothed in fine linen, white and clean, were following Him on white horses. From His mouth comes a sharp sword, so that with it He may strike down the nations, and He will rule them with a rod of iron; and He treads the wine press of the fierce wrath of God, the Almighty. And on His robe and on His thigh He has a name written, "KING OF KINGS, AND LORD OF LORDS." Then I saw an angel standing in the sun, and he cried out with a loud voice, saying to all the birds which fly in midheaven, "Come, assemble for the great supper of God, so that you may eat the flesh of kings and the flesh of commanders and the flesh of mighty men and the flesh of horses and of those who sit on them and the flesh of all men, both free men and slaves, and small and great." And I saw the beast and the kings of the earth and their armies assembled to make war against Him who sat on the horse and against His army. And the beast was seized, and with him the false prophet who performed the signs in his presence, by which he deceived those who had received the mark of the beast and those who worshiped his image; these two were thrown alive into the lake of fire which burns with brimstone. And the rest were killed with the sword which came from the mouth of Him who sat on the horse, and all the birds were filled with their flesh. (Rev. 19:11–21)

The passage above shows that Christ's return will be one that entails great physical destruction and death. For those who are not Christ's own, it will be a terrifying and terrible event. It will bring the judgment, separating the saved from the unsaved (Matt. 25:31–46).[2]

One of the purposes of the second coming is to right wrongs in history. Many injustices have been committed by the opponents of God to His people that have not been vindicated in history. Scripture says that God will avenge His people at the second coming (2 Thess. 2:5–10). The second coming enables believers to not become overwhelmed by injustice because they know that perfect justice will be instituted at Christ's return.

Some people believe that the second coming has already occurred, and there are even some within Christendom who make such claims. This interpretation is known as preterism (Latin for "past"). Preterists argue that major prophetic portions of Scripture, such as some passages in the books of Matthew and Revelation, were fulfilled in events surrounding the A.D. 70 destruction of Jerusalem by the Romans. In its fullest expression, preterism teaches that Jesus Christ has already returned to earth and that we are now living in the kingdom age.

Not all preterists believe that the final second coming of Christ has occurred, but they all do believe that Christ has returned in some form. Extreme preterists, or consistent preterists as they prefer to be known, believe that all future Bible prophecy was fulfilled in the destruction of Jerusalem in A.D. 70. If there is a future second coming, they believe, the Bible does not talk about it. This puts them in the unorthodox position of denying not only the second coming but also the bodily resurrection of believers.[3]

The reality that there will be a second coming is a truth that affects every person who has ever lived or will ever live. It is not a Hollywood special-effects production, a religious raving, a psychological paranoia, or monastery mysticism. It is a spectacular reality that will one day occur and it cannot be avoided. Regardless of the direction in which civilization drifts in any era, the end of human history is in the hands of God. Because history is moving toward the goal of Christ's return, Christians proclaim the promise of

Christ recorded in Revelation 22:20 by the apostle John who wrote, "'Yes, I am coming quickly.' Amen. Come, Lord Jesus."

31. Is the return of Jesus physical or spiritual?

The second coming of Christ is a physical and bodily return that will be clearly visible to all. Scripture tells us that the return of Jesus will be sudden, personal, and visible to all. It will be a physical return. It is not simply a spiritual return to the heart and psyche of the believer. The first coming of Jesus to earth at His incarnation and birth was physical, and so, too, will be His second coming (Heb. 9:28). Dr. John Walvoord astutely notes:

> Though it is true that Christ is present everywhere and indwells every Christian, bodily he has remained in heaven. At the Second Coming he will return bodily to earth. Just as the Ascension was a bodily ascension into heaven, so the Second Coming will be a bodily return to earth. The angels who met the disciples after the ascension of Christ told them, "This same Jesus, who has been taken from you into heaven, will come back in the same way you have seen him go into heaven" (Acts 1:11). Jesus went into heaven bodily and visibly in the clouds. His second coming will have all these same characteristics.[4]

If Christ's second coming were not physical but merely spiritual, it would not be a *second* coming. Christ has already come spiritually in the form of His indwelling presence and through the Holy Spirit. For Him to come again as He promised and as Scripture foretells is different from His first coming that was also physical and bodily. In accordance with biblical descriptions, the second coming of Jesus Christ must be a personal, physical, and visible return. It will be the culmination of history. Human history will culminate and end, not as poets and scientists have declared (with a whimper or a bang) but with the return of the Lord Jesus Christ.

32. What is the relationship between the first and second comings of Jesus?

The Bible depicts the life and ministry of Jesus Christ as revolving around two major phases. Titus 2:11–14 speaks of Christ's two appearances on earth. The first phase is related to His coming in humiliation to die for the sins of humanity. The second phase is when He will come in power and glory to reign over all humanity. The first coming of Jesus is when He gave Himself for our sin and His second coming is when He will return in glory.

> For the grace of God has appeared, bringing salvation to all men, instructing us to deny ungodliness and worldly desires and to live sensibly, righteously and godly in the present age, looking for the blessed hope and the appearing of the glory of our great God and Savior, Christ Jesus, who gave Himself for us to redeem us from every lawless deed, and to purify for Himself a people for His own possession, zealous for good deeds. (Titus 2:11–14)

Philippians 2 provides great insight into the meaning and purpose of Christ's two advents:

> Have this attitude in yourselves which was also in Christ Jesus, who, although He existed in the form of God, did not regard equality with God a thing to be grasped, but emptied Himself, taking the form of a bond-servant, and being made in the likeness of men. Being found in appearance as a man, He humbled Himself by becoming obedient to the point of death, even death on a cross. For this reason also, God highly exalted Him, and bestowed on Him the name which is above every name, so that at the name of Jesus EVERY KNEE WILL BOW, of those who are in heaven and on earth and under the earth, and that every tongue will confess that Jesus Christ is Lord, to the glory of God the Father. (Phil. 2:5–11)

Additionally, Hebrews 9:28 is a single verse that explains and contrasts Christ's two comings. The writer of Hebrews says, "so Christ also, having been offered once to bear the sins of many, will appear a second time for salvation without reference to sin, to those who eagerly await Him." The two comings are linked in history, in prophecy, and in the plan of God.

33. What will happen when Jesus returns?

The return of Christ will be followed by a series of judgments and then the inauguration of the millennial kingdom—the one-thousand-year reign of Christ upon the earth. Just as Noah's flood recorded in Genesis 6–8 was a bridge from the old world to the new, so the judgments at the second coming will be the cataclysmic hinge between our current era and the tribulation to the radically new conditions of the millennium. The second coming and the judgments that will accompany it are closely related. The judgments that occur immediately following the second coming initiate the schedule for the millennium. The following are the specific judgments that occur either right before the second coming, at the return of Jesus, or shortly thereafter:

- Judgment of Babylon, the great harlot (Rev. 17–18; 19:2–3)
- Judgment of the armies and nations at Armageddon (Rev. 19:11–21)
- Judgment of the Gentile nations (Joel 3:1–3; Matt. 25:31–46)
- Judgment of the beast or antichrist (Rev. 19:19–20)
- Judgment of the false prophet (Rev. 19:20)
- Judgment of Satan (Rev. 20:1–3)
- Judgment of Old Testament saints (Dan. 12:1–3)
- Judgment of tribulation saints (Rev. 20:4–6)
- Judgment of living Jews (Ezek. 20:34–38)

It is important to remember that when we say "the second coming" of Christ, we are not talking about the rapture that occurs prior to the second coming. The rapture is most clearly presented in 1 Thessalonians 4:13–18. It is characterized in the Bible as a "translation coming" (1 Cor. 15:51–52; 1 Thess. 4:15–17) in which Christ comes *for* His church. The second advent is Christ returning with His saints, descending from heaven to establish His earthly kingdom (Zech. 14:4–5; Matt. 24:27–31). There are many terms used in the New Testament that speak of Christ's coming. Most are used to refer to both the second coming and the rapture, even though they are separate events. A study of the context determines which a given writer has in mind.

The rapture and the second coming are two distinct and separate events in both their character and timing. A pretribulational perspective (the rapture occurs before the tribulation) has them clearly separated by the seven-year tribulation (the seventieth week of Dan. 9). The prophetic timeline of Daniel 9:24–27 and 2 Thessalonians 2 places the tribulation after the rapture and just before the second coming. Some Christians believe that the rapture and second coming will occur after the tribulation and either simultaneously or very close together. This latter position is known as posttribulationism. However, careful and consistent observation of the biblical distinctions, terminology, history, and nuances leads to a pretribulational perspective that clearly distinguishes the two events.

It is important to note the difference between the second coming and the earlier event of the rapture of the church. Note the following contrasts that distinguish the two events:

Rapture and Second Coming Contrasts

1. Translation of all believers	1. No translation at all
2. Translated saints go to heaven	2. Translated saints return to earth
3. Earth not judged	3. Earth judged and righteousness established

4. Imminent, any moment, signless	4. Follows definite predicted signs, including tribulation
5. Not in the Old Testament	5. Predicted often in Old Testament
6. Believers only	6. Affects all men
7. Before the day of wrath	7. Concluding the day of wrath
8. No reference to Satan	8. Satan bound
9. Christ come *for* His own	9. Christ comes *with* His own
10. He comes in the *air*	10. He comes to the *earth*
11. He claims His bride	11. He comes with His bride
12. Only His own see Him	12. Every eye shall see Him
13. Tribulation begins	13. Millennial kingdom begins

Based upon a comparison of these events, one can note the distinct differences in their character.[5]

34. Will Jesus rule from Jerusalem in a future millennium?

The messianic prophecies of the Old Testament clearly present a portrait of the Messiah as a king who will reign. For example, Isaiah 9:6 proclaims "the government will rest on His shoulders." Similarly, in Micah 5:2, we read that the Messiah will be born in Bethlehem where "from you One will go forth for Me to be ruler in Israel."

Isaiah 11:1–5 foretells of the Messiah who will come from the family of David and rule the nation Israel with righteousness and absolute justice. This passage is a clear prophecy of the reign of Jesus Christ during the millennium. Jesus Christ will be the focal point of all activity during the millennium. It will be His reign and His kingdom. That which was rejected at the time of His first coming will now be accepted and fully realized as He reigns on earth for one thousand years. But how do we know it is a physical reign from Jerusalem?

While the Bible contains many prophecies about Jerusalem, some of the most extensive ones are found in Isaiah 60–61, Zechariah 12 and 14, and Revelation 21–22. These passages offer some of the clearest prophetic information about the city and the future relationship of Jesus to it.[6]

During the seven-year tribulation and the military campaign of Armageddon (prior to the second coming of Jesus and the millennium), Jerusalem will experience both peace and war. According to Daniel 9:27, after the first half of the tribulation, the Antichrist will break the covenant of peace with Israel, and intense persecution and suffering will occur in Jerusalem and throughout the world. This will culminate in the Battle of Armageddon during which Jerusalem will be a focal point. Zechariah prophetically records:

> "Behold, I am going to make Jerusalem a cup that causes reeling to all the peoples around; and when the siege is against Jerusalem, it will also be against Judah. It will come about in that day that I will make Jerusalem a heavy stone for all the peoples; all who lift it will be severely injured. And all the nations of the earth will be gathered against it. In that day," declares the LORD, "I will strike every horse with bewilderment and his rider with madness. But I will watch over the house of Judah, while I strike every horse of the peoples with blindness." (Zech. 12:2–4)

At the end of the tribulation, at this critical time, Jesus the Messiah will return to the Mount of Olives in Jerusalem and destroy his enemies who have assembled in military force at Armageddon (Zech.

14:2–4, 8–9). Also, when Jesus Christ returns, Jerusalem and Israel will acknowledge Him as the Messiah (Zech. 12:10).

In the first chapter of Acts, we read of the postresurrection ascent of Jesus from the Mount of Olives after His forty days with the disciples. As the disciples stood watching the ascent, two angels appeared, telling them that Jesus would return again in the same location: "They also said, 'Men of Galilee, why do you stand looking into the sky? This Jesus, who has been taken up from you into heaven, will come in just the same way as you have watched Him go into heaven'" (Acts 1:11).

The return of Christ, or the second coming (not the rapture), was prophesied by Zechariah almost six hundred years earlier in Zechariah 14:4: "In that day His feet will stand on the Mount of Olives, which is in front of Jerusalem on the east; and the Mount of Olives will be split in its middle from east to west by a very large valley, so that half of the mountain will move toward the north and the other half toward the south." Since Christ delivered His great prophetic discourse on His second coming from the Mount of Olives, it is clearly implied that His return would be to the same location (Matt. 24–25).

Sixty years after the ascension, the apostle John also wrote of Christ's second coming to earth in Revelation 19:11–16, although the Mount of Olives is not mentioned specifically. (This coming should not be confused with the rapture that occurs seven years earlier and is recorded in 1 Thess. 4:14–17. These two comings are quite separate and distinct events.)

Isaiah 60–61 describes the glory of Jerusalem and Israel during the millennium and the ministry of Jesus during this period. It will finally be a true city of peace, for God will "make peace your administrators and righteousness your overseers. Violence will not be heard again in your land, nor devastation or destruction within your borders; But you will call your walls salvation, and your gates praise" (Isa. 60:17d–18). Isaiah continues to paint a picture of Zion's (Jerusalem's) future during Messiah's thousand-year earthly reign from the Holy City. Even though Jerusalem has been a city that has endured conflict and conquest throughout the centuries, it will eventually have lasting peace. God's restoration and blessing on Jerusalem will exceed the combined damage done throughout the ages. Its reconstruction will also bring religious and economic prosperity into her boundaries (Isa. 61:4–9).

Revelation 21 and 22 describe Jerusalem during the millennium and in the eternal state. It will be a city of joy whose gates will never be closed. Ultimately, it will be a city of purity inhabited only by believers: "And in the daytime (for there will be no night there) its gates will never be closed; and they will bring the glory and the honor of the nations into it; and nothing unclean, and no one who practices abomination and lying, shall ever come into it, but only those whose names are written in the Lamb's book of life" (Rev. 21:25–27).

Why Jerusalem instead of some other city? The return of Christ to Jerusalem will be for the purpose of judging the world and establishing His millennial kingdom; it will also establish His reign on the throne of David in fulfillment of Old Testament prophecies that assured a Messiah-King for Israel from the Davidic line. While it will be a universal rule, it will be from Jerusalem because of the Davidic throne and the spiritual restoration of Israel. Prophecy scholar John F. Walvoord writes:

> His reign over the house of Israel will be from Jerusalem (Isa. 2:1–4), and from the same location he will also reign as King of Kings and Lord of Lords over the entire earth (Ps. 72:8–11, 17–19). . . . The Millennium will be the occasion of the final restoration of Israel. At the beginning of the millennial kingdom Israel will experience her final and permanent regathering (Ezek. 39:25–29; Amos 9:15). Christ's reign over Israel will be glorious and will be a complete and literal fulfillment of all that God promised David (Jer. 23:5–8).[7]

No other city would permit the fulfillment of prophecy or allow for the rule and restoration of Israel. Jerusalem's biblical, prophetic, and worldwide significance will continue and be increased at the second coming of Christ.

PART 5

Jesus According to Extrabiblical Sources

35. Is there historical proof for the existence of Jesus?

There is more historical evidence for the man Jesus of Nazareth than for any other person in ancient history. To doubt the existence of Jesus is to bring into question the existence of great figures of history like the conqueror Alexander the Great, the philosopher Socrates, the Carthaginian general Hannibal,[1] or various Roman emperors. The rejection of the existence of Jesus has been attempted by skeptics (but rarely by recognized historians) for the last two centuries particularly, but with little success.[2] Even those who do not embrace Christianity nonetheless recognize that Jesus truly lived and that many of the aspects of His life that are recorded in the Gospels and other early sources have credibility.[3]

Alexander the Great conquered the world from Macedonia to India in ten years, lamenting that he had no more to conquer at age thirty-two. No one doubts his existence even though there exists no contemporary record of his life and works. The earliest writings we have of Alexander were four centuries after his conquests and death at Babylon (twelve years from the beginning of his conquests from Macedonia). The most substantial treatment of Alexander is found in Plutarch's *Life of Alexander*.[4] Some additional evidence is found in later writers relying on former works, their depictions of Alexander being different. Nonetheless, historians consider him a true historical personage who made a major impact on the world.

Three factors are considered by historians in vetting the historical credibility of a person: First, are there contemporary writings that provide information about the person? Second, what impact may be ascertained from their life and words? Third is the consideration of any ancillary historical and archaeological evidence that may support the claim.

Several attempts have been made over the years to discredit the historical nature of Christ's life and even His existence. A half century ago, Bertrand Russell, a well-known philosopher, attempted to discredit Christ and Christianity in his book *Why I Am Not a Christian*.[5] However, most efforts are of the nature of *The Jesus Mysteries*,[6] books laden with highly questionable inferences and faulty research, usually imposing on the first-century events in Israel and religious views and myths of later periods.

One means is to say that we can't really know that much about Jesus since the information about Him is nearly two thousand years old. William Lane Craig has revealed the inadequacy of such a criterion:

> Sometimes laymen say, "How can you know anything that happened two thousand years ago?" What they fail to understand is that the crucial time gap is not the gap between the evidence and today; rather what's important is the gap between the evidence and the original events that the evidence is about. If the gap between the events and the evidence is short, then it doesn't matter how far the event and the evidence have receded into the past. Good evidence doesn't become poor evidence just because of the passage of time! So long as the time gap between the event and the evidence for that event is short, it's just irrelevant how long

it has been to the present day. The question then is how close the sources for Jesus' life are to the time he lived.[7]

So, then, the sources do not gain less credence because they are older. Rather, the quality of the source relates not to how ancient they are but to how close they are to the actual events they record. If even one were to subscribe to the view that the New Testament documents date to the end of the first century, an unnecessary view, they still would represent understanding about Jesus, His works, words, and influence that would be fresh in the minds of many of His eyewitnesses.

Others have sought to minimize the credibility of historical sources for the life and works of Jesus. James Hannam, author of *The Genesis of Science*, sets forth on his website "Bede's Library" a sardonic portrayal of how one is able to achieve the results that deny the historicity of Jesus. He gives seven strategies of those who deny the historical Jesus, whom he calls Jesus Mythologists, which we summarize:

1. Connect Jesus with any and every mythical figure, religious story, or symbol in the ancient world so that it will be easy to find some parallel(s) with His life, so that you can claim dependence on these for the creation of your information regarding Jesus.
2. Beyond those pagan myths and stories, add also subsequent counterparts to the time of Jesus, even centuries, so that it can be claimed that information on Him actually is copied from the later period, rather than vice versa.
3. Use contemporary terminology in vogue today when translating ancient pagan sources (though they would have been unfamiliar with the ideas) that explains early Christian terms or events, even though the Christian usage is quite different from their meanings in the pagan world.
4. When Christianity and pagan religions are involved in com-

mon practices of the day (like sacred meals), act as if it a total surprise, which makes it appear as if this adds support to dependence of Christianity on paganism.

5. Make comparisons appear to be closely related even when the symbol and meaning are quite different. For example, Mithras was represented as a bull and Jesus as a lamb, quite different symbols, and the former symbolized sexuality and the latter meekness.

6. Ignore the truly major emphases of paganism in order to compare the minor elements. Include only comparisons, no matter how weak, so that there appears to be dependence.

7. Avoid modern scholarship and rely on discredited sources of the nineteenth and early twentieth-century writers. Act as if only poor researchers and charlatans or quacks disagree with you.[8]

Using such procedures, any person of antiquity can be debunked, at least to those who choose not to fairly and accurately view the evidence.

One wonders why such an effort has been made by so many to discredit Jesus. Perhaps, it is in part that because the demands of acceptance of Jesus as a true person also places a moral burden on people to accept that they are in need of His help. What, then, of the attempts to discredit the historicity of Jesus? These are feeble efforts to dispel the existence of a person who has made the greatest impact upon humanity of anyone who has ever lived. In the words of the late Jaroslav Pelikan, "Regardless of what anyone may personally think or believe about him, Jesus of Nazareth has been the dominant figure in the history of Western culture for almost twenty centuries. If it were possible, with some sort of supermagnet, to pull up out of that history every scrap of metal bearing at least a trace of his name, how much would be left? It is from his birth that most of the human race dates its calendars, it is by his name that millions curse and in his name that millions pray."[9]

Though generally viewed as a skeptic, historian Will Durant gives a fitting tribute to the historical study of the man Jesus, when he writes, "That a few simple men should in one generation have invented so powerful and appealing a personality, so lofty an ethic and so inspiring a vision of human brotherhood, would be a miracle far more incredible than any recorded in the Gospels. After two centuries of Higher Criticism the outlines of the life, character, and teaching of Christ, remain reasonably clear, and constitute the most fascinating feature in the history of Western man."[10]

36. How does Jesus relate to the Dead Sea Scrolls?

There are no specific references to the historical Jesus among the Dead Sea Scrolls discovered at Qumran in Israel, but the Essene community who lived there for approximately two hundred years had a vivid interest in the coming Messiah promised by the prophets in the Hebrew Scriptures.[11]

There is no evidence whatsoever that either Jesus or John the Baptist lived at Qumran or even visited it, though it is highly likely that they were at least familiar with this religious group in the desert near the Dead Sea. Though Jesus is unlikely to have had associated with the Essenes in the Judean desert, He may have had contact with the thousands of less radical Essenes who lived in the city of Jerusalem.

What is important about the matter of Jesus and Qumran, and the Essenes in general, is that the scrolls at Qumran reveal a very similar perspective of the ministry, power, death, and maybe even resurrection of the Messiah, as we see them fulfilled in the life of Jesus, the true Messiah of Israel.

For example, Matthew 28:18 speaks of Jesus having received all authority in heaven and earth, while Mark 4:41 has the statement, "Who then is this, that even the wind and the sea obey Him?" This perspective of Messiah is preserved for us in a fragment designated 4Q521 1–2: ". . . [the hea]vens and the earth will obey His Messiah.

[The sea and all th]at is in them." Similarly, Matthew 11:4–5 records the Messiah Jesus' words to confirm His identity to John: "Go and report to John what you hear and see: The BLIND RECEIVE SIGHT and the lame walk, the lepers are cleansed and the deaf hear, the dead are raised up, and the POOR HAVE THE GOSPEL PREACHED TO THEM." Jesus believes these types of miracles should convince John, even in his desperate moment of despair, that He truly was the Messiah to come. Such views of Messiah are also supported at Qumran, where a fragment reads: "[His] Holy [Messiah] will not be slow [in coming]. [When He comes] then He will heal the sick, resurrect the dead, and to the poor announce glad tidings" (4Q521 10, 12).

Another important fragmentary document at Qumran reads much like what is found in Luke 1:32–33: "He will be great and will be called the Son of the Most High; and the Lord God will give Him the throne of His father David; and He will reign over the house of Jacob forever, and His kingdom will have no end." The fragment (4Q246 I:6–9, II:5–7), shares similar wording: ". . . shall be great upon the earth. [O King] All shall make [peace] and all shall serve [him, and he] shall be called [son of] the [gr]eat [God], and by his name shall he be named. . . . He shall be hailed the Son of God, and they shall call him Son of the Most High. As comets (flash) to the sight, so shall their kingdom. For (some) year[s] they shall rule upon the earth and shall trample everything (under foot); people shall trample upon people, city upon ci[t]y, . . . until there arises the people of God, and everyone rests from the sword" (trans. Joseph Fitzmyer). Two other documents have been found that are in agreement with New Testament teaching about Jesus, namely, His death and resurrection. The Pierced Messiah Fragment (4Q285, 4–5) seems to speak about the Messiah (called Branch of David) being put to death with piercing. A recent stela was found near the Dead Sea in Jordan that is written in the same manner as the scrolls, and it speaks, very possibly, of Messiah being raised to life in three days.[12]

One does not need to consider that the New Testament authors borrowed from the elusive and secluded Essenes at Qumran who penned these documents above; actually, they are too different to be merely copied. Rather, there was a common expectation of what Messiah was to be, one that Jesus fulfilled and was understood by John the Baptist, and the crowds, that He indeed was the Messiah.

Additionally, the apostles shared similar understandings of the Old Testament prophecies with the Jews at Qumran and many rabbis (see question 9). At Qumran two kinds of documents were found, the Hebrew Scriptures and what is known as sectarian scrolls that contained the theology and practices of this Jewish sect. The latter religious documents present the Messiah as a prophet, priest, and a king (though there seem to be two Messiahs in the view of some of the literature).

Neither Jesus nor His disciples had association with the Jews at Qumran, but the men at Qumran shared with the entire Jewish community certain beliefs about the Messiah (possibly due to the Hebrew Scriptures and the influence of the *Book of Enoch* in this period). These beliefs were not dependent on their works, nor that of the writer of Enoch, but they were certainly in agreement with them in general terms since they were the way that all of these understood the Hebrew Scriptures. Moreover, they all approached the Scriptures in the same way, namely, a belief in the literal interpretation of Scripture.

37. Are there ancient sources for the existence of Jesus?

Jesus in Graeco-Roman Sources

There is considerable evidence that Jesus lived. Biblical, Jewish, and Graceo-Roman writings attest to this fact.[13] Moreover, certain aspects of the New Testament accounts are confirmed in the extrabiblical sources, such as Jesus' death under Pontius Pilate by crucifixion.

The Roman historian Tacitus (ca. A.D. 56–117), who was a critic of the emperor Nero, most likely speaks of followers of Jesus, the Christ, in his *Annals of Imperialo Rome* (ca. A.D. 108), as he discusses Nero's blaming of Christians for the burning of Rome. He says, "Their originator, Christus had been executed in Tiberius's reign by the Procurator of Judaea, Pontius Pilatus."

Pliny the Younger (d. ca. A.D. 112) was a governor in the Roman province of Bithynia and was a friend of the emperor Trajan. Having arrested some Christians, he gave them opportunity to recant, something to which Trajan later agrees. Pliny, in his letter to Trajan, said that the Christians he had arrested confess "Christ as a god."

Suetonius (d. ca. A.D. 135) served in the court of the Roman emperor Hadrian and was also a historian. In his *Life of Claudius*, he writes, "As the Jews were making constant disturbances at the instigation of Chrestus [Latin variant of Greek *Christos*], he [Claudius] expelled them from Rome" (25:4).

In the second or third century A.D., a letter was written from a Syrian named Mara bar Serapion that speaks of the death of Jesus and calls Jesus the Jewish king. The account is not as strong as some but may give evidence of Jesus' death.

Lucian (ca. A.D. 125–180) was a Greek writer, rather than Roman, but is in the time period we are discussing. He criticized Christians for being naive by using the story of a man named Proteus who duped Christians as he traveled among them. In so doing, though, he gives evidence of the Christian beliefs that Jesus lived in Israel, was crucified because of His teaching, had disciples who followed Him, and that Jesus was worshipped as a god.

Jesus in Jewish Sources

There are primarily three sources in Jewish literature that speak of Jesus. The first, the historian Josephus, is dispassionate about his references, whereas the latter two, the Talmud and the critic Celsus, are hostile to Jesus.

Josephus (ca. A.D. 37–100) has two references to the Christ in his *Antiquities of the Jews* that refer to Jesus as the Christ. The first, called the *Testimonium*,[14] appears to have been altered by a Christian copier at some time in its history, but most scholars recognize that there are comments from the pen of Josephus that acknowledge that Jesus was a historical person who died under the rule of Pontius Pilate. Following is the passage, with the suspected interpolations in brackets:

> About this time arose Jesus a wise man [if indeed it be right to call Him a man]. For He was a doer of marvelous deeds, and a teacher of men who gladly receive the truth. He drew to himself many persons, both of the Jews and also of the Gentiles. [He was the Christ.] And when Pilate upon the indictment of the leading men among us, had condemned him to the cross, those who loved him at the first did not cease to do so [for he appeared to them alive on the third day-the godly prophets having foretold these and ten thousand other things about him]. And even to this day the race of Christians, who are named from him, has not died out.[15]

At another place in the *Antiquities*, Josephus refers to Jesus as the "so-called" Christ: ". . . he [Annas the younger] convened a judicial session of the Sanhedrin and brought before it the brother of Jesus the so-called Christ—James by name—and some others, whom he charged with breaking the law and handed over to be stoned to death."[16] This account is virtually certain a genuine comment from Josephus and mentions the Lord's brother James, the leader of the Jerusalem church, a person mentioned by Josephus elsewhere. Josephus also mentions John the Baptist several times.

The second source for the life of Jesus is found in the Babylonian Talmud. In this tractate, the Talmud says that Jesus was hanged on Passover Eve, and that forty days earlier a charge was made regarding the apostasy of Jesus and announcing for anyone who wanted to support Him to give testimony. The text continues that Jesus was not to be spared because He was near to kingship. Last of all, there is a list of five of Jesus' disciples (there seems to be no knowledge of the remainder), with confusion as to their names.[17]

Last of all is the account of Origen's *Against Celsus*, in which this Alexandrian father wrote against a Gentile critic of Christ and Christianity, but one who seems very aware of Jewish theology and the claims regarding Jesus by Christians. Thus, we include him in this section on Jewish sources. Celsus claimed that Jesus was actually an illegitimate child who acquired the knowledge of sorcery in Egypt and claimed to be a god who had come in human form. In arguing against Christianity, Celsus said that were God to have come into human form, the divine nature would be altered. Moreover, if God wanted to rescue all people, then why would He come to just one place in the world? Origin's lengthy response to Celsus in *Against Celsus* provides the interested reader the manner and types of arguments that Christians made against their detractors in the second century.

38. What are the Christian sources for the life and teachings of Jesus?

Understandably, Jesus is found throughout all of the Christian materials of the late first century forward. The question that usually arises among critics of Jesus is whether early fathers and theologians of the church viewed Him as God. There are many hundreds of instances where this belief in His deity may be found, and we will provide only a few examples:[18]

Clement of Rome (A.D. 100), the earliest of the apostolic fathers,[19] said, "We must think of Jesus as we do of God." Another early father, Ignatius (ca. A.D. 100), said of Jesus that He was "God Himself came among us in human form."

In the middle of the second century A.D., Justin Martyr (known as such because of his martyrdom) said, "the Father of the universe has a Son; who being the logos and First-begotten is also God."[20] An important late second-century father, Clement of Alexandria (A.D. 170), when speaking about Jesus, asserted, "Our educator, O children, resembles His Father, God, whose son He is. He is without sin, without blame, without passion of soul, God immaculate in form of man accomplishing His Father's will."[21] At another place Clement said, "Both as God and as a man, the Lord renders us every kind of help and service. As God He forgives sin, as man He educates us to avoid sin completely."[22] The father of the Latin church was Tertullian, who was both lawyer and theologian. His brilliant mind sought to grasp the mystery of God and gave us the word *trinitas*, Latin for "three in one," and from which we derive our term *Trinity*. He said of Jesus, "the only God has also a Son, his Word who has proceeded from himself, by whom all things were made and without whom nothing has been made: that this was sent by the Father into the virgin and was born of her both man and God. Son of Man, Son of God."[23] The first great theologian of the church was Irenaeus, a theologian from Syria, who went to become bishop at Lyons in Gaul (France), and in referencing Jesus said, "in order that to Christ Jesus, our Lord, and God, and Savior, and King, according to the will of the invisible Father."[24]

In the early third century Hippolytus, a Latin theologian, spoke of the apostle John's teaching regarding Jesus in John 1:1: "And the blessed John in the testimony of his gospel, gives us an account of this economy and acknowledges this word as God, when he says, 'In the beginning was the Word, and the Word was with God and the Word was God.' If then the Word was with God and was also God, what follows? Would one say that he speaks of two Gods? I shall not indeed speak of two Gods, but of one; of two persons however, and of a third economy, the grace of the Holy Ghost."[25]

Fathers from the third century on, particularly from the Council of Nicea, spoke of Jesus as God, though among some heterodox believers, how the Son related His Father in regard to the attributes of deity differed. None believed He was only a man.

39. Did Paul start a new religion?

Some have argued that Paul began a new religion, but when comparing how Jesus viewed Himself and how other apostles portrayed Him in their writings, Paul is in accord with what we know of Jesus. He considered the person Jesus to be both God and man, in the true sense of these words.

The apostle believed that Jesus was the eternal God, dwelling among humans. In Romans 9:5, he speaks of Jesus as "God, blessed forever." In a hymn to Christ (probably borrowed by Paul), He says that Jesus shared the very nature of God (Phil. 2:6) before taking upon Himself manhood, and that He declared that all would fall on their knees to declare that Jesus, the Messiah, is Yahweh (Phil. 2:9–10), quoting from Isaiah 45:23. In Romans 1:3–4, Paul proclaimed that Jesus was declared (not made) to be the Son of God by His resurrection.

Paul had considerable knowledge of the historical Jesus. He identified Jesus with the Jesus of Nazareth. He said that Jesus was an Israelite (Rom. 9:4), that He was of the tribe of David (Rom. 1:3), that He lived under the law (Gal. 4:4), that He had a brother by the name of James (Gal. 1:19), that He was poor (2 Cor. 8:9), that He ministered among the Jews (Rom. 15:8), that He had twelve disciples (1 Cor. 15:5), that He instituted a last supper (1 Cor. 11:23–25), and that He was crucified, buried, and was raised from the dead (1 Cor. 1:23; 15:4; 2 Cor. 13:4; Gal. 3:1, 13).

Paul was also aware of traditions about the character of Jesus. He knew of His meekness and gentleness (2 Cor. 10:1), His obedience to God (Rom. 5:19), His endurance (2 Thess. 3:5), His grace (2 Cor. 8:9), His love (Rom. 8:35), His total denial of Himself (Phil. 2:6–8), His righteousness (Rom. 5:18), and His sinlessness (2 Cor. 5:21).

Paul was aware of many quotes from the teachings of Jesus, though these would probably have been based on oral tradition rather than Gospel accounts, in view of the early date of his writings. In 1 Corinthians 7:10–11 he quotes the teaching of Jesus on divorce that may be found in Mark 10:2–12. Quoting an analogy that is found in Luke 10:7, he says that a preacher of the gospel has a right to have his material needs met (1 Cor. 9:14; 1 Tim. 5:18). The words of institution of the Eucharist—as given by Christ in Matthew 26:26–29, Mark 14:22–25, and Luke 22:14–23—are found in 1 Corinthians 11:23–32, when Paul teaches the Corinthians the importance of the Lord's Supper.

Finally, the apostle Paul bases his teaching on the teachings of Christ in Romans 12:1–15:7 (cf. Matt. 5–7), 2 Corinthians 10:1 (cf. Matt. 11:29), Romans 15:1 (cf. Mark 8:34), Romans 15:3 (ca. Mark 10:45), and Philippians 2:7 (cf. Luke 22:27 and John 13:4–17).

40. How does Jesus relate to the Gnostic gospels?

The origin of Gnosticism is a question of much debate. Some have attempted to view it as a contemporary of Jewish Christianity and so as a competing form of Christianity in the first century. Such a view has virtually no support but much supposition and plenty of popular media to advocate it. In reality, early Christianity relies on the Old Testament theology as taught by Christ and on the teachings of Christ as they were taught and passed on by the apostles. Several decades after the body of belief that was taught by Jesus and the apostles was known, heretical views of Christ emerged that were opposed by the apostle John and the church father Ignatius. These views are later found in a more developed form in the Gnosticism that developed in the second century in Egypt, along with heretical perspectives of God, man, sin, and salvation. Gnosticism was syncretistic, pulling together aspects of Greek philosophical thought about the nature of the material and immaterial world, Jewish views of ritual and Old Testament history and persons, Persian Zoroastrian ideas of ethical dualism, symbols of Christianity and the person of Christ.

Until the middle of the twentieth century, little was known of Gnosticism other than what a few of the church fathers wrote in their rebuttals, particularly Irenaeus in *Against Heresies*. Then in 1945 in upper Egypt at Nag Hammadi, a library of ancient documents was found, containing several Gnostic gospels (among other writings) that spoke of Jesus, often in unfamiliar ways as compared to the Gospels of the first century. These works have never been accepted by the church as canonical, nor representative of the life and teachings of Jesus as preserved by the apostles and their followers. Many modern skeptics have embraced them, however, because they offer an alternative to the theology of Christ found in the New Testament, and they discount the notion of an inspired New Testament text written by eyewitnesses and their associates.

So what is the portrayal of Jesus in the Gnostic documents? Read the words of Irenaeus:

> Among these, Saturninus came from Antioch . . . like Menander, he taught that there is one Father (*unum patrern incognitum*), who made angels, archangels, virtues, powers; and that the world, and everything in it, was made by seven angels. Humanity was also created by these angels . . . He also declared that the Saviour was unborn, incorporeal and without form, asserting that he was seen as a human being in appearance only. The God of the Jews, he declares, was one of the angels; and because the Father wished to destroy all the rulers (*Principes*), Christ came to destroy the God of the Jews.[26]

According to Gnosticism, then, Jesus was not the God of the Old Testament but He instead came from the ultimate spirit [not mentioned by Irenaeus in this quote] to destroy the God of the Old Testament. Moreover, Jesus was not a corporeal being but only a spirit who looked to be flesh and bone. John speaks to this heresy, though not to developed Gnosticism that may have formed around three decades later, when he says that for one to deny that Jesus came, and remains, in the flesh, such a denial is not of God (1 John 4:2–3).[27]

Jesus and Alternative Viewpoints

41. What did ancient heresies teach about Jesus?

There were a number of heresies regarding the person of Messiah Jesus, rejecting either His full humanity or His full deity, beginning toward the last portion of the first century A.D. through the fifth century. We will first examine heresies that challenged His deity and then His humanity.

Heresies Relating to Full Deity

At first, among a Jewish group known as the Ebionites (meaning poor, possibly of spirit), Ebionism held the view that Jesus was only a man who had the Spirit of God dwelling in Him, though possibly in an *adoptionist* sense in which the divine spirit substituted for the human spirit of Jesus. The Ebonites also believed that obedience to the law was needed for salvation.

In the fourth century a heresy arose known as Arianism. Arius was a bishop in Alexandria who taught that Jesus was divine but did not share the same undivided attributes of God with the Father. He declared that Jesus was a created being. Arius was opposed by a deacon in Alexandria named Athanasius, a person careful in thinking and committed to the teaching of Scripture. Athanasius argued that the Son was eternally begotten of the Father and shared the exact undivided essence of God with the Father. As the creed says, the Son is "God of very God, begotten, not made." The view of Athanasius became enshrined in the Nicene Creed (A.D. 325) and confirmed at Constantinople (Nicene II) in A.D. 381. The final vote at Nicea was approximately 300 to 2 for the creed.

Another heresy that developed in the second century A.D. and continued into the fifth century is known as modalism. Those who advocate this heresy argue that the Godhead (or divine being) has one person, not three. The most common view is what was expressed by Sabellius, who said that the Logos was the Father in creation, the Son in redemption, and the Holy Spirit in the church. Connected to this view is the erroneous belief that the Father suffered on the cross. Modalists believed that there is one person who plays different parts in the drama of human history. This is contrary to the faith of the church throughout its history that has affirmed that Father, Son, and Holy Spirit are one God, each having the totality of the divine nature without division but being distinct (not separate) from each other.

Heresies Relating to Full Humanity

Gnosticism denied the true humanity of Jesus. Borrowing on the Greek perspective that the body was secondary to the spirit, even a prison of a sort, Gnostics extended the dichotomy of Plato and believed that Jesus only appeared to be a man of flesh. In reality, they taught He entered into the world to help release humans from human frailty with secret knowledge of salvation. Jesus was a portion of the ultimate divine spirit who sneaked into the world through the virgin in what was thought to be a fleshly birth, and finally became spirit again to reunite with the divine spirit. This mixture of Eastern thought and Christian ideas was opposed by the Christian theologian Irenaeus in his *Against Heresies*.

An earlier heresy of Cerinthus has the rejection of Jesus' true humanity in common with Gnosticism's rejection of Jesus' true humanity, but Cerinthus held to a belief in adoptionism, in which the divine Logos joined with the man Jesus at His baptism, but left the man Jesus before His death. In other words, there was no true incarnation of the Son.

Heresies Relating to a Confusion of the Humanity and Deity

Last of all, two heresies that developed regarding the relation of the human and divine in Jesus arose in the late fourth century and early fifth century. One father said that there were two consciousnesses or persons in Christ, so that the mind of Christ was separated between the divine and human natures. Nestorius was declared a heretic for this view, though he did deny that he held to it. In reaction to Nestorius was the bishop Eutyches, who said that Christ did not have two distinct natures, but in reality had a blending of the divine and human into a new nature, a God-man, rather than God and man.

What must be maintained by Christians is the belief that the eternal Son of God, who is fully God in every sense, sharing the totality of the divine essence, entered into human history without surrendering any of His divine attributes. On earth, He was both fully God and fully man, even as He is now, one person in two natures.

Heresy	Date (A.D.)	Viewpoint
Ebionism	1st–4th century	A Jewish philosophy of the first and early second century that believed Jesus was the Messiah spoken about in the Hebrew Scriptures but that He was only a human, not God.
Cerinthianism	ca. 100	Cerinthus believed that the Logos descended on the human Jesus at His baptism and departed before His death on the cross.

Heresy	Date (A.D.)	Viewpoint
Gnosticism	2nd–4th century	Gnosticism took a variety of forms, but in general argued for a god different from the God of the Old Testament. It believed that Jesus gave only the appearance of being a human being.
Valentinianism	ca. 100–ca. 160	Most sophisticated of the Gnostic views, arguing for a number of emanations from the Supreme Father. Jesus was an aeon who appeared to be in bodily form but was actually an immaterial being from outside the world. The Savior was to bring enlightenment rather than forgiveness.
Marcionism	ca. 110–160	Most well known of the heretics of the early church. He was anti-Semitic, and believed in a god of the Old Testament and a god of the New Testament who were in conflict with each other. Jesus was a spiritual entity sent to the earth. Marcion developed a canon of Scripture that excluded the Old Testament, and included only Luke, Acts, and the Pauline letters.
Manichaeism	ca. 210–276	Mani considered himself the prophet of the final religion, in the line of other prophets, including Jesus. He was influenced by Gnosticism and believed in two spheres of existence: light and darkness (the former ruled by God and the latter by Satan).
Monarchianism	2nd century	Monarchianism appeared in two forms. The first is Dynamic Monarchianism, in which God is unipersonal, and Jesus only a man. Modalistic Monarchianism said that the Logos of God manifested Himself in three different forms, Father, Son and Holy Spirit, but was only one person.

Heresy	Date (A.D.)	Viewpoint
Arianism	4th century	View of Arius, a bishop in Alexandria, that the Logos was a being created by the Father, and although he had divine aspects, was not of the same essence as the Father.
Apollonarianism	4th–early 5th century	Apollonarianism argued that the Logos indwelt a human Jesus, so that Jesus was not a fully human being.
Eutychianism	late 4th–middle 5th century	Eutychianism believed that Jesus did not have two distinct natures but His divine and human natures were blended into a new, third nature.
Nestorianism	late 4th–middle 5th century	Nestorius said that the divine and human natures were entirely separate from each other, resulting in two persons and two natures.

Source: Adapted from H. Wayne House, *The Jesus Who Never Lived* (Eugene, OR: Harvest House, 2008), 257–59. Used by permission.

42. How is Jesus viewed in Islam?

Travels of Jesus in Distant Lands

Muslims do not believe that Jesus died on the cross, but rather, according to some Islamic traditions, Jesus traveled among the Arabs after the supposed death of Judas on the cross. Supposedly He went to Damascus for about two years, and Paul encountered Him near the city. He is alleged to have preached to the king of Nisibis in southeastern Turkey, and another story says that He went to Afghanistan where He performed miracles. Still others, relying on Sura 23:50 of the Qur'an, state that He went to what is present-day Pakistan. Allegedly, Mary and Jesus lived there and Mary was buried there. (However, as will be seen below, many other Muslims believe Jesus ascended to heaven without far-reaching travels.)

Claims of Islam About Jesus

Jesus has a unique and revered role in Islam but it is not the Christian view of Jesus Christ.[1] Islam began in the middle of the seventh century A.D., but Muslims have claimed that in reality it is their monotheist faith from which Judaism and Christianity came. The patriarch Abraham (Ibrahim), dating to 2000 B.C., is prominent in the Qur'an and viewed as the archetype of the perfect Muslim— what is known as a *hernif*, someone who intrinsically knows and believes there is only one God. So, too, is Moses (Musa) given a special place in Islam along with various prophets, and finally, Jesus. Islam means "submission" and a Muslim means "one who submits." According to Islam, Abraham and other Old Testament righteous men surrendered to God and so they were Muslim men who surrendered to the one God, Allah.

The fact, however, that Muslims believe in one God does not prove that they worship the God of Abraham.[2] Muhammad came to believe in one God rather than adopt the polytheism around him in Arabia, probably because of his contact with Jews and Christians. He seems to have gotten his knowledge of biblical characters in this manner and, particularly, his knowledge of Jesus. He even encouraged his followers in the early stage of the development of Islam to go to people of the Book should they want religious knowledge, something that changed in his post-Mecca period. The only Christian Bible that existed in the mid-seventh century A.D. would be those codices and manuscripts that we have access to today. Islam teaches a number of things about Jesus that have partial agreement with what is taught in the New Testament, but as one can imagine, certain elements reflect Islamic perspectives. Unfortunately, the Christianity that Muhammad came into contact with was not orthodox but heretical (primarily Arianism). The result of this was a view of Christianity (and Judaism) that was largely syncretistic, eclectic, and heretical.

According to Islam, Jesus was the greatest prophet until Muhammad, and He is recognized as the Messiah (*Al-Masih*, close to *ha-mashiach* in Hebrew), the word of Allah, and the son of Mary, a virgin (Sura 3:42 et al; see 21:91; 66:12; 23:50; Mary is the only woman mentioned in the Qur'an). Jesus is known as *'Isa* in Arabic (not very close to His Hebrew name *Yeshua'*, even though they are cognate languages). Supposedly the Gospel (*Injil*) of Jesus (Sura 19:31; 4:169; 3:48; 4:46) was lost and corrupted by later Christians, so that the Qur'an is the only reliable guide to the teachings of Jesus. The Qur'an teaches that He was a worker of miracles in His ministry (Sura 5:112–114) and said to predict the coming of Muhammad (Sura 61:6).[3] Jesus is said to have come to call Israel to obey Allah. Last of all, Jesus is considered to be a coming judge of those Christians and Jews who failed to embrace the truth of Islam. At His coming, it is thought, that all Jews and Christians will believe the Islamic teaching of Jesus. He then will eventually die and be buried beside Muhammad. Islam denies that Jesus was divine and that Jesus was crucified on a cross.[4] It also denies the resurrection. Rather, "according to Islamic tradition, when the Jews sought to kill Jesus, God outwitted them by projecting his likeness onto someone else who they mistakenly crucified. Meanwhile, he caused Jesus to ascend to the second or third heaven, where he is still alive."[5]

There is a smattering of truth in these aforementioned Islamic perspectives of Jesus, namely, that He was born of a virgin, that He was a worker of miracles, that He came to call Israel to repentance, that He promised another helper that the Father would send, and that He is coming as a righteous judge. Unfortunately for those who adhere to Islam, the biblical truths are different from the advocacy of Islam, and for the Christian they are far more glorious, as we await our God and Savior, Messiah Jesus (Titus 2:13; 2 Peter 1:1–3).

43. How is Jesus viewed in Eastern religions?

Readers may be surprised to find that there is a tradition of Jesus in the Far East.[6] Such surprise is probably for two reasons. One is the great distance from the sites of the life and ministry of

Christ and the spread of the gospel recorded in the New Testament. Second is the great difference between Judeo-Christian beliefs and those of the East.

Those who believe that Jesus has been influenced by Eastern religion and philosophical thought overcome these two obstacles through two means. First, it is believed that at the time He began His public ministry in His early to mid thirties, Jesus actually traveled to the Far East and back to Nazareth after the time of His sojourn in Egypt. Second, it is argued that Jesus held much in common with the philosophy of Eastern personages like Krishna or the Buddha and this is found in His teaching. Third, some believe that the teaching about Jesus is borrowed from Hinduism aspects of the story of Krishna.

Is there any evidence that Jesus went to the East to travel and study in lands of India and/or China? There is no credible evidence that Jesus ever ventured from Israel to travel the great distance to India, China, or even a closer location like Persia. This is merely wishful thinking on the part of those who want to deny the uniqueness of the events surrounding Jesus and His teaching.[7] We do know that He traveled across the Jordan River to Perea and as far north as Mt. Hermon, but beyond this, His travels were largely around the Sea of Galilee and to Jerusalem for the feasts. It is true that Thomas probably went to India to preach the gospel (possibly providing an origin to the stories), but there is no evidence that Jesus did so.

Second, are there resemblances between the teaching of Jesus and what is found in Hinduism and Buddhism? Some have alleged that there are similarities between the teaching of Jesus and Krishna and the Buddha. In what ways are they similar, according to these proponents? Krishna is the beginning, middle, and end of all beings, and Jesus is the beginning and ending of all things. The biblical text sets forth Jesus as an eternal being, while Hinduism sees Krishna as an originator of all beings. Supposedly the birth narrative of Jesus in Luke 2:25–35 is like the story of Asita in the

Bhagavad-Gita, but a simple look at *Bhagavad-Gita* 10:12–13 shows no parallel to Luke's account.[8] Jesus spoke often of the kingdom of God and, supposedly, the *Bhagavad-Gita* makes similar comments. Yet when one reads the accounts, the Hindu sense of kingdom is quite different from the biblical sense, both to its nature and the basis of one's entrance.[9] When one looks in the life of Krishna for those necessary elements of Jesus' teaching found in the Gospels, one loses the "virgin birth, incarnation, sinless life, crucifixion, descent into hell, resurrection, ascension to heaven."[10]

The only similarity between the teaching of Buddha and Jesus relates to compassion for people and the need to alter the contemporary religious teaching. Much more could be given, but the life and teachings of Jesus are greatly different from Krishna or Buddha.

Third, is the story of Jesus built upon the story of Krishna? This is a common myth, and some have even claimed that Eusebius and Augustine believed as much. Yet these two fathers of the church never made such a claim, and their words are misunderstood.[11] According to Hinduism, Krishna, the eighth manifestation of the god Vishnu, was born between 1200 and 900 B.C. Jesus is said to be a further manifestation.

After acknowledging that they began their ministries around the same age, both fasted, and lived a simple life, the similarity of Jesus and Buddha largely ends there. The meaning of these similarities diverges significantly. While Buddha received enlightenment sitting under a tree, Jesus received His commission in a public act with the lighting of the Holy Spirit as a dove at His baptism and the voice of the Father from heaven. Jesus' fasting related to resisting temptation and not self-contemplation as Buddha.

While it is certainly true that the gospel of Christ was carried to the East in the decades and centuries after the ascension of Jesus Christ, Christ and Christianity are incompatible with Hinduism and Buddhism (and the recent New Age thought based on Eastern mysticism).[12] The latter focuses on contemplation and denial of the physical world, rejection of the existence of sin as a basis for eternal judgment, and the need for salvation through the death of a perfect man to bring forgiveness of sin. Jesus represents the fulfillment of the Hebrew Bible with its belief in a real physical world, a transcendent God, and the need of forgiveness to be saved. Jesus and Eastern religion are worlds apart.[13]

44. How does Jesus of history differ from the Jesus of religious tradition and popular media?

Would Jesus recognize how He is depicted in the popular religion of today? How has the image of Jesus changed over the many centuries since He lived on the earth? Does our manner of speaking or singing about Him or the way in which we depict Him in art in any way detract or blemish who Jesus is; are any of these blasphemous? These are questions we will briefly consider.

The iconic tradition of the Eastern church has a regulated manner in which Jesus has been painted from the early centuries of the church. The imagination of the artist is not permitted in portrayals of Jesus. The icons are more than a portrait; in fact, they are considered the "holy flesh" of Christ. In the Roman Catholic tradition, images of Jesus took a variety of forms. Sometimes He is shown on a crucifix, either in paintings or in sculpture. These works were created with worship in mind, and different images seek to express different doctrines of the church. He might be shown as a Good Shepherd, a tortured and crucified Savior, or even a bridegroom or lover. All of these ways of speaking of Jesus have come down through the last two millennia.

The great masters of the Renaissance brought their skill to portraying Jesus in art, but unlike the early icons that show a person similar to a Middle Eastern man today, the Renaissance artists and sculptors made Jesus reflect a European perspective, both in facial features and dress. He was truly made in their image. With the Reformation came a new way to look at Jesus, both in art and theology. Luther moved from the more soft and lean portrayal of

Jesus to a more robust figure. The typical manner of emphasizing the suffering of Christ gave way to an emphasis on the crucifixion itself, even by means of figures like a lamb. With Calvin came a de-emphasis on art and more focus on personal activity in worship by the words of music and preaching.

Modern images of Jesus have changed considerably since the time of the Reformation. The way in which Jesus has been viewed has been "from hero to victim, from liberator to suppressor, from serious to comedic."[14] Contemporary art has chosen to use Jesus as a social, political, and cultural symbol rather than seeking to capture a theological idea from the New Testament. By some, Jesus was even made anti-Semitic, looking very German or Aryan with rabbis surrounding Him. In other works He has been shown as a champion of the masses or social justice. The depictions are myriad.

The way in which Christian music speaks of Jesus is perhaps the most powerful contemporary tool for shaping many Christians' perspective of Jesus. In much of the Western church, hymns have been replaced with "praise songs." Originally hymns were written to teach theology regarding God, Jesus as Savior, salvation by faith, and other important doctrines. Praise songs reflect a contemporary emphasis on short stanzas and long choruses. Rather than develop-ing biblical teaching about God, Christ, and salvation, much praise music is concerned about how the singer feels about Jesus and his or her response to Him. Much of it is in the vein of secular music or religious (Christian) pop music in which the singer is in love with Jesus, though often His name is not mentioned or Jesus is a close friend. Often secular songs are made into Christian songs with little need to change the words. Even secular music got into sing-ing about Jesus or religious themes in the 1960s and 1970s, but the understanding of Jesus was minimal.

Another way in which Jesus is presented in popular culture is found in movies and film. Until *The Passion of the Christ*, Jesus was usually very European and often spoke with a British acc

Often He appeared to be a weakling or even a mystic. Some films only showed Jesus in cameo appearances as part of a larger religious film such as *Ben Hur*, while some like *King of Kings* (1961) focus on Jesus with the use of different statements of Jesus in the Gospels. Campus Crusade for Christ produced the movie *Jesus* that was largely the words of Jesus from the gospel of Luke; it has been used in evangelism throughout the world, but the actor still looks much too European. Other films, like *Jesus Christ Superstar* and *The Last Temptation of Christ*, sought to be sensational in nature and depict Jesus in less than biblical and often scandalous form.

In much of contemporary Western Christianity, sometimes broader, cultural gimmicks like WWJD (What Would Jesus Do) led to bracelets being worn by large numbers of young people who had little understanding of the Gospel accounts of Jesus and had not a clue as to what Jesus would do. They transposed what they thought Jesus should do to fit their perspective of Him, whereas He might actually act quite differently.

What has become popular is the view that everybody loves Jesus. Of course, what this means is that everyone loves the Jesus that they have created in their minds, and if the real Jesus were to be present, they would have the same kind of problems with Him as those who opposed and disliked Him in the first century.

The Jesus of the first century was a man of great integrity and forthrightness. He "called a spade a spade," as the saying goes. He called sinners to repentance and did not excuse sin, even among His disciples. He was open to forgiveness but would judge the sin and the sinner. He was fully committed to His Father's will and the mission for which He had come to the earth. He was a Jew and worshipped in the temple accordingly; this was conservative and orderly worship. He was not opposed to ritual, for He performed it in His prayers and blessings and in His practice of the feasts, including Passover. When confronted with problems, questions, and temptation, His constant appeal was to Holy Scripture, not to feelings or speculations about what He should do. He knew the Hebrew Scriptures well enough to know the plan of action or to have the proper answer to questions that were posed. Jesus was fully God and fully man in one person. He lost none of His deity to take upon Himself manhood.[15] He was a self-sacrificing Savior, and at His second coming, He will proclaim Himself King.

In an extended but significant passage, theologian Carl F. H. Henry astutely declared:

> In a day when God is caricatured by the crude images of our callous culture, Jesus Christ perfectly preserves and perpetuates the divine image. In a day when impersonal processes—quarks and quasars—are given primacy, Jesus Christ stands as the first-born of all creation and the sovereign creator of all things and powers. In a day when humanism considers history and nature haphazard, purposeless, and directionless, Christ remains the upholding and unifying principle of the universe which exists through him and for him. In a day when the world is crammed with evil, the fullness of the Godhead dwells in Jesus Christ who stands in incomparable relationships both to the Godhead and the universe. The divine essence is his; he precedes the universe in time and surpasses it in rank; he is the agent in its creation and the sustainer of it; he supplies its unity and meaning; and its final goal.[16]

Jesus Christ far exceeds any portrayals of Him in art, music, literature, film, or any other creative expression.

Popular culture has many images of Jesus. He is seen as a teacher, friend, prophet, wise man, revolutionary, healer, role model, leader, and a score of other things. Each of these has some accuracy, but none of them captures the most important thing, something that so much of popular culture fails to see and believe—Jesus Christ a Savior.

45. What is the Jesus Seminar and how has it influenced contemporary views?

Many of those reading this book have heard of the Jesus Seminar but few know much about this group and the viewpoints espoused by it. Since this book concerns Jesus, only those matters that directly relate to Him will be presented in this section; other issues regarding the Jesus Seminar are discussed in our book *Answers to Common Questions About the Bible*.

Approximately seventy persons initially made up the Jesus Seminar, though the number has varied. Most of these persons are not recognized New Testament scholars, but there have been some prominent scholars in the group such as Robert Funk, John Dominic Crossan, and Marcus Borg. Even though they have been highly favored by many in the media, and their views have been presented as established New Testament scholarship, their findings, in general, have been rejected by most New Testament scholars, both liberal and conservative. A major work produced by the group is called *The Five Gospels: The Search for the Authentic Words of Jesus*. It would surprise most people in the Christian world to know that there are five gospels rather than four; this is very important to the design of the Jesus Seminar. The fifth gospel is a quasi-Gnostic gospel of the second century made up of various alleged sayings of Jesus. Most are quite mystical in nature, though some have a familiar ring to the words of Jesus in the New Testament. Nonetheless, the Jesus Seminar has sought to establish this work as the most important genuine gospel and argues it should be dated in the middle of the first century.

What quickly becomes obvious about the participants of the Jesus Seminar is a great dislike for what the church has believed about Jesus from its inception, namely, that Jesus is God, was born of a virgin, healed the sick, and rose from the dead. Robert Funk asserts that "The Christ of creed and dogma . . . can no longer command" assent since we are modern persons. Science has "dismantled holological abodes of the gods and Satan, and bequeathed us

51. How could Jesus have been the all-knowing God and yet not know the time of His second coming?

In Mark 13:32, Jesus is on the Mount of Olives talking to Peter, James, John, and Andrew about the future, especially the tribulation era before the second coming. He tells them: "But of that day or hour no one knows, not even the angels in heaven, nor the Son, but the Father alone." Although the proximity of Christ's return may be perceived by the events that precede it (vv. 28–29), the precise moment is known only by God the Father. How can Jesus say that He, the Son, does not know the time, when He is God and God is omniscient (all-knowing)?

The confession of ignorance by Jesus ("nor the Son") was not made to define the limits or boundaries of Jesus' theological knowledge as the second person of the Trinity but to prompt the disciples to faithfulness and vigilance rather than to calculations on a calendar. The lack of knowledge is on account of the humanity of Jesus rather than the deity of Jesus. This is one of the passages in the Bible that shows the perpetual tension that exists in understanding the divine and human natures of Jesus Christ. Jesus the Son, in His earthly life and ministry, did have physical and mental limitations. Yet, at the same time, He was also deity. For example, Luke 2:52 states, "And Jesus kept increasing in wisdom and stature, and in favor with God and men." In His humanity, Jesus grew and learned, as does any person. Jesus also became thirsty and tired (Matt. 4:2; 21:18; John 4:6; 19:28) and needed the ministry of angels following the temptations by Satan while in the wilderness and before the crucifixion (Matt. 4:11; Luke 22:43). Jesus was fully God and fully human (1 Tim. 2:5).

The title "Son" used by Jesus in this passage affirms Jesus' awareness of His deity and Sonship (see also Mark 8:38), but Jesus also only exercised His divine attributes in concurrence with the Father (Mark 5:30; John 8:28–29). In His humanity, Jesus had limited knowledge. The incarnation entailed voluntary limitation of the use of the divine attributes that Jesus had as God the Son (Phil. 2:6–8). The emphasis of the passage is not the ignorance of Jesus but the need for vigilance by the disciples regardless of the circumstances or the future. The best preparation for the future is to remain alert and obedient to God (Mark 13:33, 37).

52. Did Jesus really descend into hell?

In 1 Peter 3:19–20 we read: "He [Jesus] went and made proclamation to the spirits now in prison, who once were disobedient, when the patience of God kept waiting in the days of Noah, during the construction of the ark, in which a few, that is, eight persons, were brought safely through the water." When and what did Jesus preach to spirits in prison and who were they? Peter's words about the preaching of Jesus are found in an extended passage (1 Peter 3:13–4:19) on the meaning and purpose of suffering in the lives of Christians. In these verses, Peter reminds readers of the suffering of Jesus Christ in His undeserved death and the results that came from that death. The death of Jesus was not a defeat but a spiritual victory that brought salvation to all who believe. Through His death and resurrection, Jesus was triumphant over sin, death, and Satan. Moreover, nothing can come against Christians that is beyond the power and control of Jesus Christ (1 Peter 3:22).

The triumph of Jesus in the crucifixion and resurrection is certain and not in question. What has been debated through the centuries is when and how Jesus made proclamation to spirits in prison. Even the reformer Martin Luther found this a strange verse with an obscure meaning and struggled with its exact meaning.

There are several views on this passage with combinations or variations within each view.[1] One common view is associated with the Apostles' Creed (but not the longer and more detailed Nicene Creed) in the words "he descended into hell," which implies that between the crucifixion and resurrection Jesus preached to imprisoned spirits in hell. These spirits are understood to have been either fallen angels perhaps from Genesis 6, or humans from the time of Noah or other Old Testament times, who are awaiting the final judgment of God at the end of this age. Often this proclamation is then viewed to have been one of condemnation in which Jesus said in effect "I told you so!" and announced His victory over sin and death. Others argue that Jesus descended into hell and proclaimed release to people who had repented just before they died in the flood of Noah (Gen. 6–9). Also associated with the descent into hell view, but taking a different interpretive tack, is an understanding of a second chance at salvation after death (though v. 20 limits the audience to those of Noah's day). While this passage is often cited in support of such a descent, we do not find the passage to teach such an activity (see also the comments below on Eph. 4:9). Nor is there any support in the Bible for a second chance at salvation after death (Heb. 9:27).

A second major view is that Jesus proclaimed His victory to fallen angels (probably those who had married women in Gen. 6:9), perhaps either between His death and resurrection or at some unrecorded time prior to or during His ascension into heaven (Acts 1:9). During the New Testament era, there was a strong tradition and belief within Judaism of fallen angels being kept in prison (see, for example, the nonbiblical book *1 Enoch* 10–16, 21). While there was much interest in angels during Jesus' day, there is no certainty that Peter's readers were aware of the writing and tradition of *1 Enoch*, nor is the word Greek for *spirits* in *1 Enoch* always translated to mean angelic creatures (or demons).

A third major view with a long history of support (including Augustine, Aquinas, and many during the Reformation) is that the pre-incarnate Christ preached through Noah to his generation. In this understanding, the preaching was done by Christ through the Holy Spirit and the person of Noah. Just as the Holy Spirit spoke through King David in his day (Acts 1:16; 4:25), so, too, did it happen in Noah's day while he was building the ark before the great flood. The message that was preached was one of repentance to the unbelievers of Noah's generation who refused to repent and are now in hell. The view also fits well with 1 Peter 1:11, which speaks of the pre-incarnate Christ speaking through the Old Testament prophets and with 2 Peter 2:5, in which Noah is said to be a "preacher of righteousness." One shortcoming of this view is that *spirit* is almost never used in the New Testament in reference to people. None of the interpretations is fully satisfactory and each has grammatical, lexical, or theological shortfalls, though the third view seems most consistent with the immediate context. In the context, readers of the letter are encouraged to boldly proclaim their faith in a hostile environment just as Noah did. They can be certain that regardless of how small their numbers, God will save, and Jesus Christ will ultimately triumph over evil.

What is certain is that Jesus' resurrection was confirmation of all that was prophesied in the Old Testament and that Jesus Christ "is at the right hand of God, having gone into heaven, after angels and authorities and powers had been subjected to Him" (1 Peter 3:22).

A second verse sometimes used to support the idea of Jesus descending into hell is Ephesians 4:9: "Now this expression, 'He ascended,' what does it mean except that He also had descended into the lower parts of the earth?" As noted above, the notion of a descent into hell has appeared throughout the centuries in various Christian creeds, most notably, later versions of the Apostles' Creed. But the Apostles' Creed was not written by any of the apostles or a single church council. Rather, it was developed during a five hundred–year period from A.D. 200–750, and the descent into hell phrase was very late in its incorporation into the creed. One of the verses cited for support of this teaching is Ephesians 4:9 (along with 1 Peter 3:19). But is that what Paul had in mind in this passage?

In Ephesians 4, Paul is discussing unity and diversity in the entire church and in 4:8 he summarizes Psalm 68, especially verse 18. This psalm portrays a triumphant warrior returning in glory, receiving gifts, and distributing gifts to his followers. Paul uses that imagery and says that in redeeming sinful people Jesus Christ provides spiritual liberation and then presents Christians as gifts to the universal church. Each person is unique and has different abilities and responsibilities within Christ's church (4:11–12).

In this context, verses 9–10 provide a parenthetical comment on the giving of gifts by Jesus by stating that before Jesus could ascend into heaven, He first had to descend "into the lower parts of the earth." Just as in a round-trip journey, a person must leave home before the second part of returning home, so also did Jesus have to leave heaven before returning to heaven.

"To where did Christ descend?" When Paul writes of the "lower parts of the earth," what did he mean by those words? Some interpreters have understood the descent to be Christ's descent at Pentecost as He gave spiritual gifts to the church through the Holy Spirit, but there have been three other major understandings. Many have understood the phrase to mean parts lower than the earth or under the earth, in support of a descent into Hades. Others believe Paul was saying that Jesus descended to earth, and the phrase should be read "the lower parts, namely, the earth." A third solution is that it refers to the incarnation and subsequent death of Jesus with the idea being "the earth's lower part, the grave."

This latter view fits the immediate context of the passage well. Paul is stating that the same Christ who went up into heaven in His ascension is also He who earlier came down from heaven. He descended from heaven to be born as a human. In His incarnation, He was indeed crucified, died, and buried, gloriously rising on the third day, victor over sin and death, offering spiritual liberation and salvation to all. These verses do not teach a descent into hell.

believers, how the Son related His Father in regard to the attributes of deity differed. None believed He was only a man.

39. Did Paul start a new religion?

Some have argued that Paul began a new religion, but when comparing how Jesus viewed Himself and how other apostles portrayed Him in their writings, Paul is in accord with what we know of Jesus. He considered the person Jesus to be both God and man, in the true sense of these words.

The apostle believed that Jesus was the eternal God, dwelling among humans. In Romans 9:5, he speaks of Jesus as "God, blessed forever." In a hymn to Christ (probably borrowed by Paul), He says that Jesus shared the very nature of God (Phil. 2:6) before taking upon Himself manhood, and that He declared that all would fall on their knees to declare that Jesus, the Messiah, is Yahweh (Phil. 2:9–10), quoting from Isaiah 45:23. In Romans 1:3–4, Paul proclaimed that Jesus was declared (not made) to be the Son of God by His resurrection.

Paul had considerable knowledge of the historical Jesus. He identified Jesus with the Jesus of Nazareth. He said that Jesus was an Israelite (Rom. 9:4), that He was of the tribe of David (Rom. 1:3), that He lived under the law (Gal. 4:4), that He had a brother by the name of James (Gal. 1:19), that He was poor (2 Cor. 8:9), that He ministered among the Jews (Rom. 15:8), that He had twelve disciples (1 Cor. 15:5), that He instituted a last supper (1 Cor. 11:23–25), and that He was crucified, buried, and was raised from the dead (1 Cor. 1:23; 15:4; 2 Cor. 13:4; Gal. 3:1, 13).

Paul was also aware of traditions about the character of Jesus. He knew of His meekness and gentleness (2 Cor. 10:1), His obedience to God (Rom. 5:19), His endurance (2 Thess. 3:5), His grace (2 Cor. 8:9), His love (Rom. 8:35), His total denial of Himself (Phil. 2:6–8), His righteousness (Rom. 5:18), and His sinlessness (2 Cor. 5:21).

Paul was aware of many quotes from the teachings of Jesus, though these would probably have been based on oral tradition rather than Gospel accounts, in view of the early date of his writings. In 1 Corinthians 7:10–11 he quotes the teaching of Jesus on divorce that may be found in Mark 10:2–12. Quoting an analogy that is found in Luke 10:7, he says that a preacher of the gospel has a right to have his material needs met (1 Cor. 9:14; 1 Tim. 5:18). The words of institution of the Eucharist—as given by Christ in Matthew 26:26–29, Mark 14:22–25, and Luke 22:14–23—are found in 1 Corinthians 11:23–32, when Paul teaches the Corinthians the importance of the Lord's Supper.

Finally, the apostle Paul bases his teaching on the teachings of Christ in Romans 12:1–15:7 (cf. Matt. 5–7), 2 Corinthians 10:1 (cf. Matt. 11:29), Romans 15:1 (cf. Mark 8:34), Romans 15:3 (ca. Mark 10:45), and Philippians 2:7 (cf. Luke 22:27 and John 13:4–17).

40. How does Jesus relate to the Gnostic gospels?

The origin of Gnosticism is a question of much debate. Some have attempted to view it as a contemporary of Jewish Christianity and so as a competing form of Christianity in the first century. Such a view has virtually no support but much supposition and plenty of popular media to advocate it. In reality, early Christianity relies on the Old Testament theology as taught by Christ and on the teachings of Christ as they were taught and passed on by the apostles. Several decades after the body of belief that was taught by Jesus and the apostles was known, heretical views of Christ emerged that were opposed by the apostle John and the church father Ignatius. These views are later found in a more developed form in the Gnosticism that developed in the second century in Egypt, along with heretical perspectives of God, man, sin, and salvation. Gnosticism was syncretistic, pulling together aspects of Greek philosophical thought about the nature of the material and immaterial world, Jewish views of ritual and Old Testament history and persons, Persian Zoroastrian ideas of ethical dualism, symbols of Christianity and the person of Christ.

Until the middle of the twentieth century, little was known of Gnosticism other than what a few of the church fathers wrote in their rebuttals, particularly Irenaeus in *Against Heresies*. Then in 1945 in upper Egypt at Nag Hammadi, a library of ancient documents was found, containing several Gnostic gospels (among other writings) that spoke of Jesus, often in unfamiliar ways as compared to the Gospels of the first century. These works have never been accepted by the church as canonical, nor representative of the life and teachings of Jesus as preserved by the apostles and their followers. Many modern skeptics have embraced them, however, because they offer an alternative to the theology of Christ found in the New Testament, and they discount the notion of an inspired New Testament text written by eyewitnesses and their associates.

So what is the portrayal of Jesus in the Gnostic documents? Read the words of Irenaeus:

> Among these, Saturninus came from Antioch . . . like Menander, he taught that there is one Father (*unum patrern incognitum*), who made angels, archangels, virtues, powers; and that the world, and everything in it, was made by seven angels. Humanity was also created by these angels . . . He also declared that the Saviour was unborn, incorporeal and without form, asserting that he was seen as a human being in appearance only. The God of the Jews, he declares, was one of the angels; and because the Father wished to destroy all the rulers (*Principes*), Christ came to destroy the God of the Jews.[26]

According to Gnosticism, then, Jesus was not the God of the Old Testament but He instead came from the ultimate spirit [not mentioned by Irenaeus in this quote] to destroy the God of the Old Testament. Moreover, Jesus was not a corporeal being but only a spirit who looked to be flesh and bone. John speaks to this heresy, though not to developed Gnosticism that may have formed around three decades later, when he says that for one to deny that Jesus came, and remains, in the flesh, such a denial is not of God (1 John 4:2–3).[27]

Jesus and Alternative Viewpoints

41. What did ancient heresies teach about Jesus?

There were a number of heresies regarding the person of Messiah Jesus, rejecting either His full humanity or His full deity, beginning toward the last portion of the first century A.D. through the fifth century. We will first examine heresies that challenged His deity and then His humanity.

Heresies Relating to Full Deity

At first, among a Jewish group known as the Ebionites (meaning poor, possibly of spirit), Ebionism held the view that Jesus was only a man who had the Spirit of God dwelling in Him, though possibly in an *adoptionist* sense in which the divine spirit substituted for the human spirit of Jesus. The Ebonites also believed that obedience to the law was needed for salvation.

In the fourth century a heresy arose known as Arianism. Arius was a bishop in Alexandria who taught that Jesus was divine but did not share the same undivided attributes of God with the Father. He declared that Jesus was a created being. Arius was opposed by a deacon in Alexandria named Athanasius, a person careful in thinking and committed to the teaching of Scripture. Athanasius argued that the Son was eternally begotten of the Father and shared the exact undivided essence of God with the Father. As the creed says, the Son is "God of very God, begotten, not made." The view of Athanasius became enshrined in the Nicene Creed (A.D. 325) and confirmed at Constantinople (Nicene II) in A.D. 381. The final vote at Nicea was approximately 300 to 2 for the creed.

Another heresy that developed in the second century A.D. and continued into the fifth century is known as modalism. Those who advocate this heresy argue that the Godhead (or divine being) has one person, not three. The most common view is what was expressed by Sabellius, who said that the Logos was the Father in creation, the Son in redemption, and the Holy Spirit in the church. Connected to this view is the erroneous belief that the Father suffered on the cross. Modalists believed that there is one person who plays different parts in the drama of human history. This is contrary to the faith of the church throughout its history that has affirmed that Father, Son, and Holy Spirit are one God, each having the totality of the divine nature without division but being distinct (not separate) from each other.

Heresies Relating to Full Humanity

Gnosticism denied the true humanity of Jesus. Borrowing on the Greek perspective that the body was secondary to the spirit, even a prison of a sort, Gnostics extended the dichotomy of Plato and believed that Jesus only appeared to be a man of flesh. In reality, they taught He entered into the world to help release humans from human frailty with secret knowledge of salvation. Jesus was a portion of the ultimate divine spirit who sneaked into the world through the virgin in what was thought to be a fleshly birth, and finally became spirit again to reunite with the divine spirit. This mixture of Eastern thought and Christian ideas was opposed by the Christian theologian Irenaeus in his *Against Heresies*.

An earlier heresy of Cerinthus has the rejection of Jesus' true humanity in common with Gnosticism's rejection of Jesus' true humanity, but Cerinthus held to a belief in adoptionism, in which the divine Logos joined with the man Jesus at His baptism, but left the man Jesus before His death. In other words, there was no true incarnation of the Son.

Heresies Relating to a Confusion of the Humanity and Deity

Last of all, two heresies that developed regarding the relation of the human and divine in Jesus arose in the late fourth century and early fifth century. One father said that there were two consciousnesses or persons in Christ, so that the mind of Christ was separated between the divine and human natures. Nestorius was declared a heretic for this view, though he did deny that he held to it. In reaction to Nestorius was the bishop Eutyches, who said that Christ did not have two distinct natures, but in reality had a blending of the divine and human into a new nature, a God-man, rather than God and man.

What must be maintained by Christians is the belief that the eternal Son of God, who is fully God in every sense, sharing the totality of the divine essence, entered into human history without surrendering any of His divine attributes. On earth, He was both fully God and fully man, even as He is now, one person in two natures.

Heresy	Date (A.D.)	Viewpoint
Ebionism	1st–4th century	A Jewish philosophy of the first and early second century that believed Jesus was the Messiah spoken about in the Hebrew Scriptures but that He was only a human, not God.
Cerinthianism	ca. 100	Cerinthus believed that the Logos descended on the human Jesus at His baptism and departed before His death on the cross.

Heresy	Date (A.D.)	Viewpoint
Gnosticism	2nd–4th century	Gnosticism took a variety of forms, but in general argued for a god different from the God of the Old Testament. It believed that Jesus gave only the appearance of being a human being.
Valentinianism	ca. 100–ca. 160	Most sophisticated of the Gnostic views, arguing for a number of emanations from the Supreme Father. Jesus was an aeon who appeared to be in bodily form but was actually an immaterial being from outside the world. The Savior was to bring enlightenment rather than forgiveness.
Marcionism	ca. 110–160	Most well known of the heretics of the early church. He was anti-Semitic, and believed in a god of the Old Testament and a god of the New Testament who were in conflict with each other. Jesus was a spiritual entity sent to the earth. Marcion developed a canon of Scripture that excluded the Old Testament, and included only Luke, Acts, and the Pauline letters.
Manichaeism	ca. 210–276	Mani considered himself the prophet of the final religion, in the line of other prophets, including Jesus. He was influenced by Gnosticism and believed in two spheres of existence: light and darkness (the former ruled by God and the latter by Satan).
Monarchianism	2nd century	Monarchianism appeared in two forms. The first is Dynamic Monarchianism, in which God is unipersonal, and Jesus only a man. Modalistic Monarchianism said that the Logos of God manifested Himself in three different forms, Father, Son and Holy Spirit, but was only one person.

Heresy	Date (A.D.)	Viewpoint
Arianism	4th century	View of Arius, a bishop in Alexandria, that the Logos was a being created by the Father, and although he had divine aspects, was not of the same essence as the Father.
Apollonarianism	4th–early 5th century	Apollonarianism argued that the Logos indwelt a human Jesus, so that Jesus was not a fully human being.
Eutychianism	late 4th–middle 5th century	Eutychianism believed that Jesus did not have two distinct natures but His divine and human natures were blended into a new, third nature.
Nestorianism	late 4th–middle 5th century	Nestorius said that the divine and human natures were entirely separate from each other, resulting in two persons and two natures.

Source: Adapted from H. Wayne House, *The Jesus Who Never Lived* (Eugene, OR: Harvest House, 2008), 257–59. Used by permission.

42. How is Jesus viewed in Islam?

Travels of Jesus in Distant Lands

Muslims do not believe that Jesus died on the cross, but rather, according to some Islamic traditions, Jesus traveled among the Arabs after the supposed death of Judas on the cross. Supposedly He went to Damascus for about two years, and Paul encountered Him near the city. He is alleged to have preached to the king of Nisibis in southeastern Turkey, and another story says that He went to Afghanistan where He performed miracles. Still others, relying on Sura 23:50 of the Qur'an, state that He went to what is present-day Pakistan. Allegedly, Mary and Jesus lived there and Mary was buried there. (However, as will be seen below, many other Muslims believe Jesus ascended to heaven without far-reaching travels.)

Claims of Islam About Jesus

Jesus has a unique and revered role in Islam but it is not the Christian view of Jesus Christ.[1] Islam began in the middle of the seventh century A.D., but Muslims have claimed that in reality it is their monotheist faith from which Judaism and Christianity came. The patriarch Abraham (Ibrahim), dating to 2000 B.C., is prominent in the Qur'an and viewed as the archetype of the perfect Muslim—what is known as a *hernif*, someone who intrinsically knows and believes there is only one God. So, too, is Moses (Musa) given a special place in Islam along with various prophets, and finally, Jesus. Islam means "submission" and a Muslim means "one who submits." According to Islam, Abraham and other Old Testament righteous men surrendered to God and so they were Muslim men who surrendered to the one God, Allah.

The fact, however, that Muslims believe in one God does not prove that they worship the God of Abraham.[2] Muhammad came to believe in one God rather than adopt the polytheism around him in Arabia, probably because of his contact with Jews and Christians. He seems to have gotten his knowledge of biblical characters in this manner and, particularly, his knowledge of Jesus. He even encouraged his followers in the early stage of the development of Islam to go to people of the Book should they want religious knowledge, something that changed in his post-Mecca period. The only Christian Bible that existed in the mid-seventh century A.D. would be those codices and manuscripts that we have access to today. Islam teaches a number of things about Jesus that have partial agreement with what is taught in the New Testament, but as one can imagine, certain elements reflect Islamic perspectives. Unfortunately, the Christianity that Muhammad came into contact with was not orthodox but heretical (primarily Arianism). The result of this was a view of Christianity (and Judaism) that was largely syncretistic, eclectic, and heretical.

According to Islam, Jesus was the greatest prophet until Muhammad, and He is recognized as the Messiah (*Al-Masih*, close to *ha-mashiach* in Hebrew), the word of Allah, and the son of Mary, a virgin (Sura 3:42 et al; see 21:91; 66:12; 23:50; Mary is the only woman mentioned in the Qur'an). Jesus is known as *'Isa* in Arabic (not very close to His Hebrew name *Yeshua'*, even though they are cognate languages). Supposedly the Gospel (*Injil*) of Jesus (Sura 19:31; 4:169; 3:48; 4:46) was lost and corrupted by later Christians, so that the Qur'an is the only reliable guide to the teachings of Jesus. The Qur'an teaches that He was a worker of miracles in His ministry (Sura 5:112–114) and said to predict the coming of Muhammad (Sura 61:6).[3] Jesus is said to have come to call Israel to obey Allah. Last of all, Jesus is considered to be a coming judge of those Christians and Jews who failed to embrace the truth of Islam. At His coming, it is thought, that all Jews and Christians will believe the Islamic teaching of Jesus. He then will eventually die and be buried beside Muhammad. Islam denies that Jesus was divine and that Jesus was crucified on a cross.[4] It also denies the resurrection. Rather, "according to Islamic tradition, when the Jews sought to kill Jesus, God outwitted them by projecting his likeness onto someone else who they mistakenly crucified. Meanwhile, he caused Jesus to ascend to the second or third heaven, where he is still alive."[5]

There is a smattering of truth in these aforementioned Islamic perspectives of Jesus, namely, that He was born of a virgin, that He was a worker of miracles, that He came to call Israel to repentance, that He promised another helper that the Father would send, and that He is coming as a righteous judge. Unfortunately for those who adhere to Islam, the biblical truths are different from the advocacy of Islam, and for the Christian they are far more glorious, as we await our God and Savior, Messiah Jesus (Titus 2:13; 2 Peter 1:1–3).

43. How is Jesus viewed in Eastern religions?

Readers may be surprised to find that there is a tradition of Jesus in the Far East.[6] Such surprise is probably for two reasons. One is the great distance from the sites of the life and ministry of

Christ and the spread of the gospel recorded in the New Testament. Second is the great difference between Judeo-Christian beliefs and those of the East.

Those who believe that Jesus has been influenced by Eastern religion and philosophical thought overcome these two obstacles through two means. First, it is believed that at the time He began His public ministry in His early to mid thirties, Jesus actually traveled to the Far East and back to Nazareth after the time of His sojourn in Egypt. Second, it is argued that Jesus held much in common with the philosophy of Eastern personages like Krishna or the Buddha and this is found in His teaching. Third, some believe that the teaching about Jesus is borrowed from Hinduism aspects of the story of Krishna.

Is there any evidence that Jesus went to the East to travel and study in lands of India and/or China? There is no credible evidence that Jesus ever ventured from Israel to travel the great distance to India, China, or even a closer location like Persia. This is merely wishful thinking on the part of those who want to deny the uniqueness of the events surrounding Jesus and His teaching.[7] We do know that He traveled across the Jordan River to Perea and as far north as Mt. Hermon, but beyond this, His travels were largely around the Sea of Galilee and to Jerusalem for the feasts. It is true that Thomas probably went to India to preach the gospel (possibly providing an origin to the stories), but there is no evidence that Jesus did so.

Second, are there resemblances between the teaching of Jesus and what is found in Hinduism and Buddhism? Some have alleged that there are similarities between the teaching of Jesus and Krishna and the Buddha. In what ways are they similar, according to these proponents? Krishna is the beginning, middle, and end of all beings, and Jesus is the beginning and ending of all things. The biblical text sets forth Jesus as an eternal being, while Hinduism sees Krishna as an originator of all beings. Supposedly the birth narrative of Jesus in Luke 2:25–35 is like the story of Asita in the

Bhagavad-Gita, but a simple look at *Bhagavad-Gita* 10:12–13 shows no parallel to Luke's account.[8] Jesus spoke often of the kingdom of God and, supposedly, the *Bhagavad-Gita* makes similar comments. Yet when one reads the accounts, the Hindu sense of kingdom is quite different from the biblical sense, both to its nature and the basis of one's entrance.[9] When one looks in the life of Krishna for those necessary elements of Jesus' teaching found in the Gospels, one loses the "virgin birth, incarnation, sinless life, crucifixion, descent into hell, resurrection, ascension to heaven."[10]

The only similarity between the teaching of Buddha and Jesus relates to compassion for people and the need to alter the contemporary religious teaching. Much more could be given, but the life and teachings of Jesus are greatly different from Krishna or Buddha.

Third, is the story of Jesus built upon the story of Krishna? This is a common myth, and some have even claimed that Eusebius and Augustine believed as much. Yet these two fathers of the church never made such a claim, and their words are misunderstood.[11] According to Hinduism, Krishna, the eighth manifestation of the god Vishnu, was born between 1200 and 900 B.C. Jesus is said to be a further manifestation.

After acknowledging that they began their ministries around the same age, both fasted, and lived a simple life, the similarity of Jesus and Buddha largely ends there. The meaning of these similarities diverges significantly. While Buddha received enlightenment sitting under a tree, Jesus received His commission in a public act with the lighting of the Holy Spirit as a dove at His baptism and the voice of the Father from heaven. Jesus' fasting related to resisting temptation and not self-contemplation as Buddha.

While it is certainly true that the gospel of Christ was carried to the East in the decades and centuries after the ascension of Jesus Christ, Christ and Christianity are incompatible with Hinduism and Buddhism (and the recent New Age thought based on Eastern mysticism).[12] The latter focuses on contemplation and denial of the physical world, rejection of the existence of sin as a basis for eternal judgment, and the need for salvation through the death of a perfect man to bring forgiveness of sin. Jesus represents the fulfillment of the Hebrew Bible with its belief in a real physical world, a transcendent God, and the need of forgiveness to be saved. Jesus and Eastern religion are worlds apart.[13]

44. How does Jesus of history differ from the Jesus of religious tradition and popular media?

Would Jesus recognize how He is depicted in the popular religion of today? How has the image of Jesus changed over the many centuries since He lived on the earth? Does our manner of speaking or singing about Him or the way in which we depict Him in art in any way detract or blemish who Jesus is; are any of these blasphemous? These are questions we will briefly consider.

The iconic tradition of the Eastern church has a regulated manner in which Jesus has been painted from the early centuries of the church. The imagination of the artist is not permitted in portrayals of Jesus. The icons are more than a portrait; in fact, they are considered the "holy flesh" of Christ. In the Roman Catholic tradition, images of Jesus took a variety of forms. Sometimes He is shown on a crucifix, either in paintings or in sculpture. These works were created with worship in mind, and different images seek to express different doctrines of the church. He might be shown as a Good Shepherd, a tortured and crucified Savior, or even a bridegroom or lover. All of these ways of speaking of Jesus have come down through the last two millennia.

The great masters of the Renaissance brought their skill to portraying Jesus in art, but unlike the early icons that show a person similar to a Middle Eastern man today, the Renaissance artists and sculptors made Jesus reflect a European perspective, both in facial features and dress. He was truly made in their image. With the Reformation came a new way to look at Jesus, both in art and theology. Luther moved from the more soft and lean portrayal of

Jesus to a more robust figure. The typical manner of emphasizing the suffering of Christ gave way to an emphasis on the crucifixion itself, even by means of figures like a lamb. With Calvin came a de-emphasis on art and more focus on personal activity in worship by the words of music and preaching.

Modern images of Jesus have changed considerably since the time of the Reformation. The way in which Jesus has been viewed has been "from hero to victim, from liberator to suppressor, from serious to comedic."[14] Contemporary art has chosen to use Jesus as a social, political, and cultural symbol rather than seeking to capture a theological idea from the New Testament. By some, Jesus was even made anti-Semitic, looking very German or Aryan with rabbis surrounding Him. In other works He has been shown as a champion of the masses or social justice. The depictions are myriad.

The way in which Christian music speaks of Jesus is perhaps the most powerful contemporary tool for shaping many Christians' perspective of Jesus. In much of the Western church, hymns have been replaced with "praise songs." Originally hymns were written to teach theology regarding God, Jesus as Savior, salvation by faith, and other important doctrines. Praise songs reflect a contemporary emphasis on short stanzas and long choruses. Rather than developing biblical teaching about God, Christ, and salvation, much praise music is concerned about how the singer feels about Jesus and his or her response to Him. Much of it is in the vein of secular music or religious (Christian) pop music in which the singer is in love with Jesus, though often His name is not mentioned or Jesus is a close friend. Often secular songs are made into Christian songs with little need to change the words. Even secular music got into singing about Jesus or religious themes in the 1960s and 1970s, but the understanding of Jesus was minimal.

Another way in which Jesus is presented in popular culture is found in movies and film. Until *The Passion of the Christ*, Jesus was usually very European and often spoke with a British accent.

Often He appeared to be a weakling or even a mystic. Some films only showed Jesus in cameo appearances as part of a larger religious film such as *Ben Hur*, while some like *King of Kings* (1961) focus on Jesus with the use of different statements of Jesus in the Gospels. Campus Crusade for Christ produced the movie *Jesus* that was largely the words of Jesus from the gospel of Luke; it has been used in evangelism throughout the world, but the actor still looks much too European. Other films, like *Jesus Christ Superstar* and *The Last Temptation of Christ*, sought to be sensational in nature and depict Jesus in less than biblical and often scandalous form.

In much of contemporary Western Christianity, sometimes broader, cultural gimmicks like WWJD (What Would Jesus Do) led to bracelets being worn by large numbers of young people who had little understanding of the Gospel accounts of Jesus and had not a clue as to what Jesus would do. They transposed what they thought Jesus should do to fit their perspective of Him, whereas He might actually act quite differently.

What has become popular is the view that everybody loves Jesus. Of course, what this means is that everyone loves the Jesus that they have created in their minds, and if the real Jesus were to be present, they would have the same kind of problems with Him as those who opposed and disliked Him in the first century.

The Jesus of the first century was a man of great integrity and forthrightness. He "called a spade a spade," as the saying goes. He called sinners to repentance and did not excuse sin, even among His disciples. He was open to forgiveness but would judge the sin and the sinner. He was fully committed to His Father's will and the mission for which He had come to the earth. He was a Jew and worshipped in the temple accordingly; this was conservative and orderly worship. He was not opposed to ritual, for He performed it in His prayers and blessings and in His practice of the feasts, including Passover. When confronted with problems, questions, and temptation, His constant appeal was to Holy Scripture,

not to feelings or speculations about what He should do. He knew the Hebrew Scriptures well enough to know the plan of action or to have the proper answer to questions that were posed. Jesus was fully God and fully man in one person. He lost none of His deity to take upon Himself manhood.[15] He was a self-sacrificing Savior, and at His second coming, He will proclaim Himself King.

In an extended but significant passage, theologian Carl F. H. Henry astutely declared:

> In a day when God is caricatured by the crude images of our callous culture, Jesus Christ perfectly preserves and perpetuates the divine image. In a day when impersonal processes—quarks and quasars—are given primacy, Jesus Christ stands as the first-born of all creation and the sovereign creator of all things and powers. In a day when humanism considers history and nature haphazard, purposeless, and directionless, Christ remains the upholding and unifying principle of the universe which exists through him and for him. In a day when the world is crammed with evil, the fullness of the Godhead dwells in Jesus Christ who stands in incomparable relationships both to the Godhead and the universe. The divine essence is his; he precedes the universe in time and surpasses it in rank; he is the agent in its creation and the sustainer of it; he supplies its unity and meaning; and its final goal.[16]

Jesus Christ far exceeds any portrayals of Him in art, music, literature, film, or any other creative expression.

Popular culture has many images of Jesus. He is seen as a teacher, friend, prophet, wise man, revolutionary, healer, role model, leader, and a score of other things. Each of these has some accuracy, but none of them captures the most important thing, something that so much of popular culture fails to see and believe—Jesus Christ is a Savior.

45. What is the Jesus Seminar and how has it influenced contemporary views?

Many of those reading this book have heard of the Jesus Seminar but few know much about this group and the viewpoints espoused by it. Since this book concerns Jesus, only those matters that directly relate to Him will be presented in this section; other issues regarding the Jesus Seminar are discussed in our book *Answers to Common Questions About the Bible.*

Approximately seventy persons initially made up the Jesus Seminar, though the number has varied. Most of these persons are not recognized New Testament scholars, but there have been some prominent scholars in the group such as Robert Funk, John Dominic Crossan, and Marcus Borg. Even though they have been highly favored by many in the media, and their views have been presented as established New Testament scholarship, their findings, in general, have been rejected by most New Testament scholars, both liberal and conservative. A major work produced by the group is called *The Five Gospels: The Search for the Authentic Words of Jesus.* It would surprise most people in the Christian world to know that there are five gospels rather than four; this is very important to the design of the Jesus Seminar. The fifth gospel is a quasi-Gnostic gospel of the second century made up of various alleged sayings of Jesus. Most are quite mystical in nature, though some have a familiar ring to the words of Jesus in the New Testament. Nonetheless, the Jesus Seminar has sought to establish this work as the most important genuine gospel and argues it should be dated in the middle of the first century.

What quickly becomes obvious about the participants of the Jesus Seminar is a great dislike for what the church has believed about Jesus from its inception, namely, that Jesus is God, was born of a virgin, healed the sick, and rose from the dead. Robert Funk asserts that "The Christ of creed and dogma . . . can no longer command" our assent since we are modern persons. Science has "dismantled the mythological abodes of the gods and Satan, and bequeathed us

secular heavens."[17] Former Roman Catholic priest John Dominic Crossan says that Jesus "did not and could not cure that disease or any other one."[18] More importantly, he says, "I do not think that anyone, anywhere, at any time brings dead people back to life."[19] In spite of Crossan's pitiful rejection of his former faith, he does capture the real controversy between the Jesus Seminar and historic, orthodox Christianity when he says, "Our disagreement is actually the contemporary restatement of a very, very ancient debate, one as old as Christianity itself, the fight between Catholic or Universal or Incarnational Christianity and Docetic or *Gnostic* or Spiritual Christianity."[20]

At least Crossan understands that there is a conflict of cataclysmic proportion between the two views of the world and of Jesus. There is a war of worldviews occurring in contemporary society, in which a substantive and influential group of critics wish to minimize, if not obliterate, the historic understanding of who Jesus is. In so doing, the Jesus presented in the biblical gospels of Matthew, Mark, Luke, and John has been replaced with a makeshift restructuring of His character, mission, acts, and words. It is impossible to separate faith from history, for faith must have an object. If there is no real Jesus as seen in the Gospels, then there is no real reason for the existence of Christianity. Genuine faith is not an unreasonable faith (1 Cor. 15) but is based on evidence that explains the facts. One cannot simply set aside the rise of the Gospel accounts so close to the death and resurrection of Christ. He died and rose, and if this were not so, it could easily have been disproven, so that Christianity would never have gained a foothold with a message that was counterintuitive. Second, one must explain the rise and continuance of Christianity. Persons may suffer and die for what they believe to be true, but they will not do so for what they know to be false.

PART 7

Jesus and Difficult Issues in the Bible

46. How could Jesus have been with God and yet be God?

John 1:1 says, "In the beginning was the Word, and the Word was facing (the) God, and the Word was God." This short verse is packed full of wonderful, theological truth that is carefully written in Greek by the apostle John.

The first clause indicates that the Word (Logos) was not created at the beginning of the creation. When the beginning began (so to speak), the Word already was. This Word was facing God. Two points need clarification in the second clause, namely, the meaning of *with*, found in the KJV, and who was being faced. The Greek language can express at least three senses of *with* (association). One Greek word, *syn*, conveys a relational association such as "being together," or "accompaniment," among other shades of meaning. Another word is *meta*, which is often indistinguishable from *syn* but can express "in the company of" another. The word used in John 1:1 is the Greek word *pros*, which indicates the idea of "direction," or "orientation toward someone" or "something." It could be translated in this verse "toward God," but "facing" seems to be the best rendering. This reflects John 1:18, in which the Son is said to be in the bosom of the Father and thus, unlike no one else (since none has seen the face of God), the Son is able to declare Him. The Logos (Son) who is eternal, as is the Father, was facing (the) God. The Greek has the article here for the purpose of expressing identity, similar to pointing one's finger at someone or something. Here God is the Father of the eternal Son, a relationship developed through the book of John: "Now, Father, glorify Me together with Yourself, with the glory which I had with You before the world was" (John 17:5). We see a very similar expression by the same author regarding Jesus and the Father in his first epistle: "What was from the beginning, what we have heard, what we have seen with our eyes, what we have looked at and touched with our hands, concerning the Word of Life—and the life was manifested, and we have seen and testify and proclaim to you the eternal life, which was with the Father and was manifested to us—" (1 John 1:1–2). Here John identifies the person that the Logos is facing (same Greek word for *with*) as the Father. Consequently the Son is facing the Father; they are two distinct persons. The latter is unquestionably God, but what of the Son who faces the Father? The last clause of John 1:1 clarifies this matter. The Greek says that the "Word was God." How could the Logos both face God and yet be God? This may be a problem to some who deny the deity of Christ, but the problem does not reside in the grammar of the Greek language. Had the clause in Greek said, "and the Word was (the) God," there would be a major contradiction. Since it does not contain an article (and Greek has no indefinite article), it refers to the quality of the Word, and not to His identity. The construction means "whatever it means to be the being God, the Word is this." The Father and the Son are distinct as persons, and yet are both truly God.

47. How can Jesus be eternal and yet the firstborn of creation?

Colossians 1:15 and Revelation 3:14 give the appearance in many translations as indicating that Jesus had a beginning. Such is not the case, which is caused by a misunderstanding and sometimes poor translation of these texts. Let us examine each one separately.

Colossians 1:15 reads, "He is the image of the invisible God, the firstborn of all creation" (Col. 1:15). Some have taken the latter statement about the Son to say that He was the first thing born at the time of creation. The Greek word for *firstborn* is *protokokos*. It can carry both an active and passive sense. The passive sense speaks of order of birth, the first one born; the active sense speaks of special status. One must also consider whether the word that follows *firstborn* is the object of this noun or the subject. If it is the object, it would be translated as the NKJV translates it, "He is the image of the invisible God, the firstborn over all creation" (Col. 1:15 NKJV). He does not come out of creation (subjective sense) but is the one who gives birth to creation (objective sense), and in the NKJV meaning, has a status "over" creation. That this is the proper understanding of verse 15 is made plain in the following verses when Paul writes, "For by Him all things were created, both in the heavens and on earth, visible and invisible, whether thrones or dominions or rulers or authorities—all things have been created through Him and for Him. He is before all things, and in Him all things hold together" (Col. 1:16–17). This meaning is in accord with John 1:3, where the text says that "All things came into being through Him, and apart from Him nothing came into being that has come into being."

The text of Revelation has a similar solution as Colossians 1:15. The Scripture provides appellations of Jesus such as "The Amen, the faithful and true Witness, the Beginning of the creation of God" (Rev. 3:14). The point of contention is the last title, "the Beginning of the creation of God." This either means that Jesus was the first thing that God (the Father) created, or that He was the "beginner" of God's creation. In this latter sense, the Greek word *arche* (beginning) may express the concept of origin. Here it takes as its object (called an objective genitive) the word *creation*. The text is in concert with the teaching of the New Testament, evincing the eternal nature of the Son, showing that He is before all creation as the Creator.

48. What does it mean that Jesus "emptied Himself"?

Jesus Christ has always existed as the second person of the Trinity (John 1:1; 8:58). Along with God the Father (the first person) and God the Holy Spirit (the third person), Jesus is God. He existed throughout eternity past and all of the Old Testament era. But at the right time in God's plan, He became a man, a real human person (Gal. 4:4). When this happened at His birth, He was fully God and fully man. Amazingly, He did not cease to be God; He was God in human flesh. Christ became human. It is this event that the apostle Paul discusses in Philippians 2:5–11 when he encourages Christians to live a lifestyle of humility, imitating Jesus Christ.

Using the imagery of pouring out the contents of a jar or jug, Paul says that Jesus emptied Himself; He divested Himself of something. What? Jesus temporarily emptied Himself of His manner of existence as equal to God. He did not set aside His deity and divine characteristics. Rather, He temporarily left heaven to come to earth, take on human form, and die on a cross for the sins of all people.

When Jesus came to earth, He temporarily set aside or surrendered the independent use of His divine powers. When He used His divine attributes, He did so only under the control of the Holy Spirit and in accordance with the Father's will.

When Paul says Jesus took the form of servant, the sense of the word *took* is not that Jesus exchanged something but, rather, that He added something. He added human personhood alongside His deity. In His person, there was not a subtraction of deity but an addition of humanity. Jesus added the limitations of humanity and temporarily ceased the use of some of His divine prerogatives (Matt. 24:36). God cannot cease to be God, but He can take on additional status. The likeness that Jesus took on means that although He was a genuine man, there were aspects of His humanity that were not absolutely like other people. For example, Jesus was human, but He did not have a sin nature (Heb. 4:15).

No one likes to be humbled or humiliated. When this happens, we feel insignificant, diminished, belittled, and embarrassed. Yet from a human viewpoint, that is exactly what happened to Jesus. Giving up the status and privileges of heaven, Jesus freely took on human flesh and blood in order to serve all people by dying for them. His humility and condescension to humanity included not only His birth in Bethlehem but also His crucifixion and death in Jerusalem. Jesus left the splendor of heaven for the humility of the cross.

49. Did Jesus know that Judas would betray Him when Judas was chosen?

All four authors of the New Testament Gospels record the betrayal of Jesus by Judas (Matt. 26:47–56; Mark 14:43–52; Luke 22:47–53; John 18:2–12). Although His arrest was a surprise to many who were with Jesus at the time, it was not a surprise to Jesus. He knew He would be betrayed, and He knew that Judas was the one who would do it (Matt. 26:20–25). Jesus was fully human but He was also fully God; although in the incarnation some of His divine attributes were temporarily set aside, Jesus did not lose all divine power, as evidenced in the miracles. The fact that Jesus knew all along that Judas would be the one who would be the traitor is seen in two verses, John 6:64 and John 6:70. In these verses John writes: "'But there are some of you who do not believe.' For Jesus knew from the beginning who they were who did not believe, and who it was that would betray Him. . . . Jesus answered them, 'Did I Myself not choose you, the twelve, and *yet* one of you is a devil?'"

Jesus knew who the true believers were among those who claimed to follow Him. He knew who had superficial faith and who had true faith. Jesus had supernatural knowledge (cf. John 1:47; 2:24–25; 6:15) and yet He made a conscious and deliberate choice in selecting Judas as one of the twelve disciples.

Whereas Peter with all his shortcomings made a confession of faith in Jesus Christ (John 6:69), Judas never did make one; there is no evidence that he truly believed. Although Judas was a disciple and one of the inner circle of twelve disciples closest to Jesus, the Bible never says that he believed in Jesus as the Messiah. Like other disciples, he followed for a while but then turned away (John 6:66). Judas had all the outward appearances of a true believer. He even had a role of great responsibility among the disciples as the one who kept the common funds for them (John 12:6). His actions were correct, but his heart was not. Earlier in His ministry, Jesus had spoken of such people and their fate at the last judgment (Matt. 7:21–23). Later, after Jesus' death, resurrection, and ascension, Paul wrote of people similar to Judas who claim to be followers of Jesus Christ but are not truly believers (Gal. 2:4; 2 Cor. 11:15, 26).

50. Could Jesus have yielded to temptation?

Jesus Christ was fully God and fully human, and these facts raise the question of the potential for sin in the life of Jesus. Since Jesus was fully human, does that mean there was a sin nature? The issue of the possibility of Jesus Christ yielding to temptation and sinning deals with the theological terms *peccability* and *impeccability*, which come from the Latin word *peccare*, "to sin." If one holds to the peccability of Jesus, then their position is that Christ could sin but didn't do so. If one argues for impeccability, then the position is that Christ could not sin. The discussion is one regarding that considers the phrases "able not to sin" and "not able to sin," meaning, was it possible for Jesus to refrain from sinning or, rather, was the nature of Jesus one such that it was impossible for Him to sin.

In accordance with the teaching of Scripture, both views acknowledge that Christ's temptations were real (Heb. 4:15), Christ experienced struggle (Matt. 26:36–46), and Christ did not sin (2 Cor. 5:21; Heb. 7:26; James 5:6; 1 Peter 2:22; 3:18; 1 John 3:5). Those who argue that Christ could sin contend that it is a logical deduction that if and since Christ was tempted, He could have sinned. To say that He could not sin is to say the temptations were not real and that, ultimately, He cannot truly sympathize with humanity. They also contend that if the possibility of sinning did not exist, then Jesus did not have freedom of will.

In response, we contend that the fact that Jesus could be and was tempted does not mean that He was susceptible to sin. By analogy we note that just because an army can be attacked, that does not mean that the army can be conquered. Because of Christ's unique nature, that which applies to us (temptation and susceptibility) does not necessarily apply to Christ. Christ can understand and sympathize with human suffering and temptation because although His temptations were not always exactly parallel to those we experience, His human nature was tried. The temptations of Christ were in every way like ours except that they did not originate in Himself; He was tempted from without, not from within. Jesus Christ manifested His free will by not sinning. Although tempted like us, Jesus never sinned. Because Jesus uniquely had two natures, fully divine and fully human, those natures existed and functioned simultaneously. Had the human nature existed independently, then theoretically Jesus could have sinned; however, it did not exist as such. Both the human and divine natures existed fully in Jesus from the moment of conception. Had Jesus sinned, the act would have involved both natures and Jesus would then not have been truly God. Our conclusion must be, therefore, that it was not possible for Jesus to sin. The temptations of Jesus were real, and He did not give in to them. He was truly tempted but did not succumb to the temptations. We must always remember that when thinking about issues such as these that we are dealing with Jesus as fully God and fully human—something that never has been and never will be true of anyone else. It is also something that we are unable to fully comprehend. We must affirm the teachings of Scripture, knowing that our understanding of them is true but incomplete.

51. How could Jesus have been the all-knowing God and yet not know the time of His second coming?

In Mark 13:32, Jesus is on the Mount of Olives talking to Peter, James, John, and Andrew about the future, especially the tribulation era before the second coming. He tells them: "But of that day or hour no one knows, not even the angels in heaven, nor the Son, but the Father alone." Although the proximity of Christ's return may be perceived by the events that precede it (vv. 28–29), the precise moment is known only by God the Father. How can Jesus say that He, the Son, does not know the time, when He is God and God is omniscient (all-knowing)?

The confession of ignorance by Jesus ("nor the Son") was not made to define the limits or boundaries of Jesus' theological knowledge as the second person of the Trinity but to prompt the disciples to faithfulness and vigilance rather than to calculations on a calendar. The lack of knowledge is on account of the humanity of Jesus rather than the deity of Jesus. This is one of the passages in the Bible that shows the perpetual tension that exists in understanding the divine and human natures of Jesus Christ. Jesus the Son, in His earthly life and ministry, did have physical and mental limitations. Yet, at the same time, He was also deity. For example, Luke 2:52 states, "And Jesus kept increasing in wisdom and stature, and in favor with God and men." In His humanity, Jesus grew and learned, as does any person. Jesus also became thirsty and tired (Matt. 4:2; 21:18; John 4:6; 19:28) and needed the ministry of angels following the temptations by Satan while in the wilderness and before the crucifixion (Matt. 4:11; Luke 22:43). Jesus was fully God and fully human (1 Tim. 2:5).

The title "Son" used by Jesus in this passage affirms Jesus' awareness of His deity and Sonship (see also Mark 8:38), but Jesus also only exercised His divine attributes in concurrence with the Father (Mark 5:30; John 8:28–29). In His humanity, Jesus had limited knowledge. The incarnation entailed voluntary limitation of the use of the divine attributes that Jesus had as God the Son (Phil. 2:6–8). The emphasis of the passage is not the ignorance of Jesus but the need for vigilance by the disciples regardless of the circumstances or the future. The best preparation for the future is to remain alert and obedient to God (Mark 13:33, 37).

52. Did Jesus really descend into hell?

In 1 Peter 3:19–20 we read: "He [Jesus] went and made proclamation to the spirits now in prison, who once were disobedient, when the patience of God kept waiting in the days of Noah, during the construction of the ark, in which a few, that is, eight persons, were brought safely through the water." When and what did Jesus preach to spirits in prison and who were they? Peter's words about the preaching of Jesus are found in an extended passage (1 Peter 3:13–4:19) on the meaning and purpose of suffering in the lives of Christians. In these verses, Peter reminds readers of the suffering of Jesus Christ in His undeserved death and the results that came from that death. The death of Jesus was not a defeat but a spiritual victory that brought salvation to all who believe. Through His death and resurrection, Jesus was triumphant over sin, death, and Satan. Moreover, nothing can come against Christians that is beyond the power and control of Jesus Christ (1 Peter 3:22).

The triumph of Jesus in the crucifixion and resurrection is certain and not in question. What has been debated through the centuries is when and how Jesus made proclamation to spirits in prison. Even the reformer Martin Luther found this a strange verse with an obscure meaning and struggled with its exact meaning.

There are several views on this passage with combinations or variations within each view.[1] One common view is associated with the Apostles' Creed (but not the longer and more detailed Nicene Creed) in the words "he descended into hell," which implies that between the crucifixion and resurrection Jesus preached to imprisoned spirits in hell. These spirits are understood to have been either fallen angels perhaps from Genesis 6, or humans from the time of Noah or other Old Testament times, who are awaiting the final judgment of God at the end of this age. Often this proclamation is then viewed to have been one of condemnation in which Jesus said in effect "I told you so!" and announced His victory over sin and death. Others argue that Jesus descended into hell and proclaimed release to people who had repented just before they died in the flood of Noah (Gen. 6–9). Also associated with the descent into hell view, but taking a different interpretive tack, is an understanding of a second chance at salvation after death (though v. 20 limits the audience to those of Noah's day). While this passage is often cited in support of such a descent, we do not find the passage to teach such an activity (see also the comments below on Eph. 4:9). Nor is there any support in the Bible for a second chance at salvation after death (Heb. 9:27).

A second major view is that Jesus proclaimed His victory to fallen angels (probably those who had married women in Gen. 6:9), perhaps either between His death and resurrection or at some unrecorded time prior to or during His ascension into heaven (Acts 1:9). During the New Testament era, there was a strong tradition and belief within Judaism of fallen angels being kept in prison (see, for example, the nonbiblical book *1 Enoch* 10–16, 21). While there was much interest in angels during Jesus' day, there is no certainty that Peter's readers were aware of the writing and tradition of *1 Enoch*, nor is the word Greek for *spirits* in *1 Enoch* always translated to mean angelic creatures (or demons).

A third major view with a long history of support (including Augustine, Aquinas, and many during the Reformation) is that the pre-incarnate Christ preached through Noah to his generation. In this understanding, the preaching was done by Christ through the Holy Spirit and the person of Noah. Just as the Holy Spirit spoke through King David in his day (Acts 1:16; 4:25), so, too, did it happen in Noah's day while he was building the ark before the great flood. The message that was preached was one of repentance to the unbelievers of Noah's generation who refused to repent and are now in hell. The view also fits well with 1 Peter 1:11, which speaks of the pre-incarnate Christ speaking through the Old Testament prophets and with 2 Peter 2:5, in which Noah is said to be a "preacher of righteousness." One shortcoming of this view is that *spirit* is almost never used in the New Testament in reference to people. None of the interpretations is fully satisfactory and each has grammatical, lexical, or theological shortfalls, though the third view seems most consistent with the immediate context. In the context, readers of the letter are encouraged to boldly proclaim their faith in a hostile environment just as Noah did. They can be certain that regardless of how small their numbers, God will save, and Jesus Christ will ultimately triumph over evil.

What is certain is that Jesus' resurrection was confirmation of all that was prophesied in the Old Testament and that Jesus Christ "is at the right hand of God, having gone into heaven, after angels and authorities and powers had been subjected to Him" (1 Peter 3:22).

A second verse sometimes used to support the idea of Jesus descending into hell is Ephesians 4:9: "Now this expression, 'He ascended,' what does it mean except that He also had descended into the lower parts of the earth?" As noted above, the notion of a descent into hell has appeared throughout the centuries in various Christian creeds, most notably, later versions of the Apostles' Creed. But the Apostles' Creed was not written by any of the apostles or a single church council. Rather, it was developed during a five hundred–year period from A.D. 200–750, and the descent into hell phrase was very late in its incorporation into the creed. One of the verses cited for support of this teaching is Ephesians 4:9 (along with 1 Peter 3:19). But is that what Paul had in mind in this passage?

In Ephesians 4, Paul is discussing unity and diversity in the entire church and in 4:8 he summarizes Psalm 68, especially verse 18. This psalm portrays a triumphant warrior returning in glory, receiving gifts, and distributing gifts to his followers. Paul uses that imagery and says that in redeeming sinful people Jesus Christ provides spiritual liberation and then presents Christians as gifts to the universal church. Each person is unique and has different abilities and responsibilities within Christ's church (4:11–12).

In this context, verses 9–10 provide a parenthetical comment on the giving of gifts by Jesus by stating that before Jesus could ascend into heaven, He first had to descend "into the lower parts of the earth." Just as in a round-trip journey, a person must leave home before the second part of returning home, so also did Jesus have to leave heaven before returning to heaven.

"To where did Christ descend?" When Paul writes of the "lower parts of the earth," what did he mean by those words? Some interpreters have understood the descent to be Christ's descent at Pentecost as He gave spiritual gifts to the church through the Holy Spirit, but there have been three other major understandings. Many have understood the phrase to mean parts lower than the earth or under the earth, in support of a descent into Hades. Others believe Paul was saying that Jesus descended to earth, and the phrase should be read "the lower parts, namely, the earth." A third solution is that it refers to the incarnation and subsequent death of Jesus with the idea being "the earth's lower part, the grave."

This latter view fits the immediate context of the passage well. Paul is stating that the same Christ who went up into heaven in His ascension is also He who earlier came down from heaven. He descended from heaven to be born as a human. In His incarnation, He was indeed crucified, died, and buried, gloriously rising on the third day, victor over sin and death, offering spiritual liberation and salvation to all. These verses do not teach a descent into hell.

Conclusion

We have presented a number of questions and answers about Jesus. But there is one final question we would like you to consider: "What is the most important thing I need to know about Jesus?" The answer is very straightforward—"Because God loves you, Jesus Christ died for your sins." John 3:16 may be the most recognized and quoted verse in the Bible: "For God so loved the world, that He gave His only begotten Son, that whoever believes in Him shall not perish, but have eternal life." We encourage you to pray, acknowledging to God that Jesus Christ died on the cross for your sins and believing and asking God for forgiveness of your sins and eternal life. If you sincerely do so, God has promised that He will hear your prayer, forgive your sins, and give you eternal life. It is the most important decision you will ever make.

A Chronological Table of the Life of Jesus Christ

Hoehner's Chronology

Birth of Jesus	winter 5/4 B.C.
Death of Herod the Great	March/April 4 B.C.
Prefects began to rule over Judea and Samaria	A.D. 6
Jesus at the temple when twelve	Passover, April 29, 9
Caiaphas became high priest	A.D. 18
Pilate arrived in Judea	A.D. 26
Commencement of John the Baptist's ministry	summer/autumn A.D. 29
Jesus' first Passover (John 2:13)	April 7, 30
John the Baptist imprisoned	A.D. 30 or 31
Jesus' second Passover	April 23, 31
Death of John the Baptist	A.D. 31 or 32
Jesus at the Feast of Tabernacles (John 5:1)	October 21–28, 31
Jesus' third Passover (John 6:4)	April 13/14, 32
Jesus at the Feast of Tabernacles (John 7:2, 10)	September 10–17, 32
Jesus at the Feast of Dedication (John 10:22–39)	December 18, 32

Jesus' final week	March 28–April 5, 33
Arrived at Bethany	Saturday, March 28
Crowds at Bethany	Sunday, March 29
Triumphal entry	Monday, March 30
Cursed fig tree and cleansed temple	Tuesday, March 31
Temple controversy and Olivet discourse	Wednesday, April 1
Jesus ate Passover meal, was betrayed, arrested, and tried	Thursday, April 2
Jesus tried and crucified	Friday, April 3
Jesus laid in the tomb	Saturday, April 4
Jesus resurrected	Sunday, April 5
Ascension of Jesus (Acts 1)	Thursday, May 14, 33
Day of Pentecost (Acts 2)	Sunday, May 24, 33

Notes

Introduction

1. Carl F. H. Henry, *God, Revelation and Authority, Vol. III, God Who Speaks and Shows* (Waco, TX: Word, 1979), 105.

Part 1: The Life and Ministry of Jesus

1. Harold W. Hoehner, *Chronological Aspects of the Life of Christ* (Grand Rapids: Zondervan, 1977), 11–14.
2. Cited in Adolf Deissman, *Light from the Ancient East*, trans. Lionel R. M. Strachan (Grand Rapids: Baker, 1965), 271. See also Paul L. Maier, *In the Fullness of Time: A Historian Looks at Christmas, Easter, and the Early Church* (San Francisco: HarperCollins, 1991), 25, 28–29.
3. For an overview of the issues surrounding December 25 and the celebration of the birth of Jesus in early Christianity, see Andrew McGowan, "How December 25 Became Christmas," at http://www.bib-arcy.org/e-features/christmas.asp (accessed July 27, 2010). See also Roger T. Beckwith, *Calendar and Chronology: Jewish and Christian* (Leiden: E. J. Brill, 1996), 71–79.
4. Hoehner, *Chronological Aspects of the Life of Christ*, 11–27.
5. Colin Brown, ed., "Jesus Christ, Nazarene, Christian," in *New International Dictionary of New Testament Theology* (Grand Rapids: Zondervan, 1977), 2:330–32.

6. Brigham Young, *Journal of Discourses* 4:259–60; Apostle Orson Hyde, *Journal of Discourses* 2:81, 210.

7. See also Darrell L. Bock, *Breaking the Da Vinci Code* (Nashville: Thomas Nelson, 2004), 47–60.

8. *Gospel of Philip*, trans. Wesley W. Isenberg, Gnostic Society-Library, Nag Hammadi Library, at http://www.gnosis.org/nag hamm/gop.html (accessed July 29, 2010).

9. Bock, *Breaking the Da Vinci Code*, 31–46.

10. For more information refuting ideas of Jesus in India, see Douglas Groothius, *Jesus in an Age of Controversy* (Eugene, OR: Harvest House, 1996), 133–51. See also H. Wayne House, *The Jesus Who Never Lived* (Eugene, OR: Harvest House, 2008), 109–24.

11. For an in-depth rebuttal of the "lost years," see Groothius, *Jesus in an Age of Controversy*, 119–32.

12. Hoehner, *Chronological Aspects of the Life of Christ*, 95.

13. Ibid., 65–93, 99. Hoehner offers the best and easiest to understand study of chronology of the Passion Week. In addition to his work, the standard work on the chronology of the Bible is Jack Finegan, *Handbook of Biblical Chronology*, rev. ed. (Peabody, MA: Hendrickson, 1998).

14. Hoehner, *Chronological Aspects of the Life of Christ*, 100.

15. Ibid., 43–44.

16. For more on the long and important history of the site and the Church of the Holy Sepulchre, see Martin Biddle, *The Tomb of Christ* (Stroud, UK: Sutton, 1999). See also Dan Bahat, "Does the Holy Sepulchre Church Mark the Burial of Jesus?" *Biblical Archaeology Review* 12:3 (May–June 1986): 26–45.

17. Darrell L. Bock and Daniel B. Wallace, *Dethroning Jesus: Exposing Popular Culture's Quest to Unseat the Biblical Christ* (Nashville: Thomas Nelson, 2007), 213. For a full rebuttal of the hypothesis, see pages 193–213. See also Gary R. Habermas, *The Secret of the Talipot Tomb: Unravelling the Mystery of the Jesus Family Tomb* (Nashville: Broadman Holman, 2007).

18. For an introduction to these methods, see Richard N. Long-enecker, *Biblical Exegesis in the Apostolic Period*, 2nd ed. (Grand Rapids: Eerdmans, 1999).

Part 2: The Person of Jesus According to the Bible

1. "Virgin, Virginity," *Encyclopedia Judaica* (Jerusalem: Keter, 1971), 16:159–60.

2. See Arnold Fruchtenbaum, *Messianic Christology* (Tustin, CA: Ariel Ministries, 1998), 32–37 and Edward E. Hindson, *Isaiah's Immanuel* (Phillipsburg, NJ: Presbyterian and Reformed Publishing, 1978).

3. Bruce M. Metzger, *The New Testament: Its Background, Growth, and Development* (Nashville: Abingdon Press, 1965), 41–42 (citing Rabbi Kaufmann Kohler, "Pharisees," in *The Jewish Encyclopedia* [New York: Funk and Wagnalls, 1905], IX:665).

4. See also Josephus, *Antiquities of the Jews* 13.5.9; 18.1.3, noted above, for more on the Pharisees.

Part 3: The Work of Jesus According to the Bible

1. Several questions come to mind when reflecting on whether Jesus is the Messiah from Yahweh. One relates to how one should understand the prophecies, or predictions, of the Old Testament regarding Messiah. Should these be taken literally? Is there a double fulfillment, with part of the prophetic passage referring to the time of the utterance and another part to the future Messiah? Do they refer to one Messiah or several? What does the position of Messiah entail? A second question concerns how the authors of the New Testament books understood the Old Testament prophecies about Messiah. What interpretive method did they use in dealing with the prophetic texts? Have Christians properly understood the Jewish manner of understanding the "fulfillment" passages? In what way did Jesus understand the Hebrew Scriptures as

referring to Himself? Thirdly, should the way in which the prophecies of the Messiah were fulfilled in His first coming be interpreted differently from the manner in which they speak of His second coming? In view of the nature of this book, we have decided not to deal with these questions in the text, but the reader may consult books such as Edward E. Hindson, *Isaiah's Immanuel*; John F. Walvood, *Jesus Christ Our Lord*; Thomas Ice and Timothy J. Demy, *Fast Facts on Bible Prophecy from A to Z*; and Arnold G. Fruchtenbaum, *Jesus Was a Jew*, and his *Messianic Christology*, all of which are listed in recommended reading.

2. Consult the comprehensive work of Eugene J. Mayhew, *Encyclopedia of Messianic Candidates & Movements in Judaism, Samaritanism, and Islam* (St. Clair Shores, MI: Cadieux & Maheux Press, 2009).

3. Though the famous leader of the revolt against Rome presented himself as the Messiah and this was fostered by the support of Rabbi Akiva, nonetheless, Simon was later assassinated by his own followers for failure to fulfill Messianic prophecies.

4. There are many prophecies in the Old Testament concerning the Messiah that are fulfilled in Jesus. For a partial listing, see H. Wayne House and Randall Price, *Charts of Bible Prophecy* (Grand Rapids: Zondervan, 2003), 53–56.

5. John Paul II, "Jesus Christ, Messiah Priest, Jesus Son and Savior: Catechesis on the Creed, part II" (February 18, 1987), 3, at http://www.vatican.va/holy_father/john_paul_ii/audiences /alpha/data/aud19870218en.html (accessed June 10, 2011).

Part 4: Jesus and the Future

1. For more on the present location and work of Jesus, see John F. Walvoord's, *Jesus Christ Our Lord* (Chicago: Moody Publishers, 1969), 219–32.

2. For more on the second coming and the prophetic events

surrounding it, see John F. Walvoord's *The Return of the Lord* (Grand Rapids: Zondervan, 1955) and John F. Walvoord, *Prophecy: 14 Essential Keys to Understanding the Final Drama* (Nashville: Thomas Nelson, 1993).

3. For a fuller refutation of preterism, see Tim LaHaye and Thomas Ice, eds., *The End Times Controversy: The Second Coming Under Attack* (Eugene, OR: Harvest House, 2003) and Mark Hitchcock and Thomas Ice, *Breaking the Apocalypse Code: Setting the Record Straight About the End Times* (Costa Mesa, CA: Word for Today, 2007).

4. John F. Walvoord, *Major Bible Prophecies* (Grand Rapids: Zondervan, 1991), 372.

5. This chart is adapted from Thomas Ice and Timothy J. Demy, *Fast Facts on Bible Prophecy from A to Z* (Eugene, OR: Harvest House, 2004). Used with permission.

6. On the prophetic significance of Jerusalem, see Randall Price, *Jerusalem in Prophecy* (Eugene, OR: Harvest House, 1998).

7. Walvoord, *Major Bible Prophecies*, 390–91.

Part 5: Jesus According to Extrabiblical Sources

1. See James Hannam's fictional treatment of the history of Hannibal with the method used by deniers of Jesus, at "Refuting the Myth That Jesus Never Existed," Bede's Library, http://www.bede.org.uk/jesusmyth.htm (last viewed May 4, 2011).

2. Few are those who believe that Jesus never existed. Even the liberal scholars still believe that Jesus was a historical person and that we have some historical evidence of Him within the New Testament.

3. Graham Stanton, *The Gospels and Jesus* (New York: Oxford University Press, 2002), xxiii. He writes: "Today nearly all historians, whether Christians or not, accept that Jesus existed and that the gospels contain plenty of valuable evidence which has to be weighed and assessed critically."

4. Plutarch, *The Life of Alexander the Great,* Modern Library

Paperback Edition, trans. John Dryden and ed. Arthur Hugh Clough (New York: Random House, 2004).

5. Bertrand Russell, *Why I Am Not a Christian* (New York: Simon & Schuster, 1957).

6. Timothy Freke and Peter Gandy, *The Jesus Mysteries* (New York: Three Rivers Press, 2001). See Wayne House's review of Freke and Gandy's book in H. Wayne House, "A Summary Critique: The Mythological Jesus Mysteries," *Christian Research Journal* 26, no. 1 (2003): 56–58.

7. William Lane Craig, *On Guard* (Colorado Springs: David C. Cook, 2010), 188.

8. Hannam, "Refuting the Myth That Jesus Never Existed."

9. Jaroslav Pelikan, *Jesus Through the Centuries* (New Haven, NJ: Yale University Press, 1985), 1.

10. Will Durant and Ariel Durant, *Caesar and Christ*, in *The Story of Civilization*, vol. 3 (New York: Simon & Schuster, 1980), x.

11. For an excellent introduction and overview of the Dead Sea Scrolls, see Craig A. Evans, *Holman QuickSource Guide to the Dead Sea Scrolls* (Nashville: Holman Reference, 2010).

12. See H. Wayne House, "The Basis in Pre-Christian Judaism and the Hebrew Scriptures for the Apostolic Preaching of the Death and Resurrection of the Messiah" (forthcoming in the *Journal of the International Society of Christian Apologetics*), in which House seeks to demonstrate similar views shared by the Essenes and the New Testament apostolic understanding of Messiah.

13. For a more complete discussion with documentation, see H. Wayne House, *The Jesus Who Never Lived* (Eugene, OR: Harvest House, 2008), 55–66, and the accompanying note. If the reader desires a short but excellent treatment of the historical sources regarding Jesus and response to critics, see the links at http://www.tektonics.org/jesusexisthub.html (accessed May 4, 2011). A more thorough analysis is found in Gary R. Habermas, *The Historical Jesus: Ancient Evidence*

for the Life of Christ (Joplin, MO: College Press Publishing, 1996).

14. See House, *The Jesus Who Never Lived*, 58–65 along with footnotes for a more complete discussion of the Jewish evidence for Jesus.

15. Quoted from ibid., 62–63. See Josephus, *Antiquities* 18.63–64.

16. Josephus, *Antiquities* 20.200.

17. See House, *The Jesus Who Never Lived*, 63–65, for a quote from the Talmud and discussion of the text.

18. Please refer to House, *The Jesus Who Never Lived* for these and other sources, with full documentation.

19. "Apostolic fathers" speaks of those persons who had contact with one or more of the apostles or their associates.

20. Justin Martyr, *First Apology* 63.15.

21. Clement of Alexander, *Christ the Educator*, chap 2.4.

22. Clement of Alexander, *Christ the Educator*, chap 3.1.

23. Tertullian, *Against Praxeas,* 2.

24. Irenaeus, *Against Heresies* I.X.1.

25. Hippolytus, *Against the Heresy of One Noetus* 14.

26. Irenaeus, *Against Heresies*, quoted in Alister McGrath, *The Christian Theology Reader* (Cambridge: Blackwell Publishers, 1995), 137.

27. For more on Jesus and Gnosticism, see Darrell L. Bock, *The Missing Gospels: Unearthing the Truth Behind Alternative Christianities* (Nashville: Thomas Nelson, 2006).

Part 6: Jesus and Alternative Viewpoints

1. For a quick Muslim perspective on Jesus, see the BBC Religions report by Tarif Khalidi, "Jesus Through Muslim Eyes," at http://www.bbc.co.uk/religion/religions/islam/beliefs/isa .shtml (accessed May 9, 2011).

   See also Tarif Khalidi, *The Muslim Jesus: Sayings and Stories in Islamic Literature* (Cambridge, MA: Harvard University Press, 2003). For an overview response from a Christian perspective and for a fuller discussion of Islamic views of Christ and Christianity, see House, *The Jesus Who Never Lived*, 125–32. See also John Ankerberg and Emir Caner, *The Truth About Islam and Jesus* (Eugene, OR: Harvest House, 2009).

2. See Timothy George, *Is the Father of Jesus the God of Muhammad?* (Grand Rapids: Zondervan, 2002).

3. The view that Jesus predicted the coming of Muhammad is beset by many problems. For a discussion of this point, see House, *The Jesus Who Never Lived*, 129–31.

4. Neal Robinson, "Jesus," in *Encyclopedia of the Qur'an*, vol. 3 (Leiden: E. J. Brill, 2003), 7. See also Cyril Glassé, "Jesus, Son of Mary," in *The Concise Encyclopedia of Islam* (San Francisco: Harper & Row, 1989), 208–9.

5. Ibid., 17.

6. For a quick perspective on Jesus in Eastern religions, see the BBC Religions reports "Jesus Through Buddhist Eyes," by Ajahn Canasiri at http://www.bbc.co.uk/religion/religions /buddhism/beliefs/jesusandbuddhism_1.shtml (accessed May 9, 2011); "Jesus in Hinduism," by Shaunaka Rishi Das at http:// www.bbc.co.uk/religion/religions/hinduism/beliefs/jesus_1 .shtml (accessed May 9, 2011); and "Jesus Through Sikh Eyes," by Nikki Singh at http://www.bbc.co.uk/religion/religions /sikhism/people/jesus.shtml (accessed May 9, 2011).

7. More about this may be found in House, *The Jesus Who Never Lived*, 111–12.

8. Ibid., 281n25. See also Eugene J. Mayhew, *Encyclopedia of Messianic Candidates and Movements in Jusaism, Samaritanism, and Islam*, 281.

9. Ibid., 116.

10. Ibid., 117.

11. Ibid., 114–15.

12. On the spread of early Christianity to the East, see Philip Jenkins, *The Lost History of Christianity* (San Francisco: HarperOne, 2008). Jenkins is very meticulous in his work and does

not fall prey to much of the revisionism of current studies in early Christianity.

13. For a fuller discussion of Jesus and Eastern religions, see House, *The Jesus Who Never Lived*, 112–25. For a look at the history and beliefs of Hinduism, Buddhism, and other Eastern religions, see H. Wayne House, *Charts of World Religion* (Grand Rapids: Zondervan, 2006), charts 57–85.

14. House, *The Jesus Who Never Lived*, 200.

15. For a more extensive treatment of Jesus and popular culture, see ibid., 191–219.

16. Carl F. H. Henry, *Christian Countermoves in a Decadent Culture* (Portland, OR: Multnomah, 1986), 89–90.

17. Robert Funk, *The Five Gospels: The Search for the Authentic Words of Jesus* (San Francisco: HarperOne, 1996), 2.

18. John Dominic Crossan, *Jesus: A Revolutionary Biography*, (San Franciso: HarperCollins, 1994), 82.

19. Ibid., 95.

20. John Dominic Crossan, "The Necessity of Historical Jesus Research for Christian Faith, Jesus at 2000," e-mail debate on the historical Jesus, Lent, 1996, quoted from http://www.markgoodacre.org/xtalk/crossan1.txt (accessed May 6, 2011).

Part 7: Jesus and Difficult Issues in the Bible

1. For a more detailed study of the passage and views, see Wayne Grudem, "Christ Preaching Through Noah: 1 Peter 3:19–20 in the Light of Dominant Themes in Jewish Literature," *Trinity Journal* 7:2 (Fall 1986): 3–31. (This article is an appendix in his commentary on 1 Peter in the *Tyndale New Testament Commentary Series*.) See also John S. Feinberg, "1 Peter 3:18–20, Ancient Mythology, and the Intermediate State," *Westminster Theological Journal* 48 (1986): 303–36.

Recommended Reading

Ankerberg, John, and Emir Caner. *The Truth About Islam and Jesus.* Eugene, OR: Harvest House, 2009.

Bahat, Dan. "Does the Holy Sepulchre Church Mark the Burial of Jesus?" *Biblical Archaeology Review* 12:3 (May–June 1986): 26–45.

Beckwith, Roger T. *Calendar and Chronology: Jewish and Christian.* Leiden: E. J. Brill, 1996.

Biddle, Martin. *The Tomb of Christ.* Stroud, UK: Sutton, 1999.

Blomberg, Craig L. *Jesus and the Gospels.* Nashville: Broadman & Holman, 1997.

Bock, Darrell L. *Breaking the Da Vinci Code.* Nashville: Thomas Nelson, 2004.

———. *Jesus According to Scripture: Restoring the Portrait from the Gospels.* Grand Rapids: Baker, 2007.

———. *The Missing Gospels: Unearthing the Truth Behind Alternative Christianities.* Nashville: Thomas Nelson, 2006.

———. *Recovering the Real Lost Gospel: Reclaiming the Gospel as Good News.* Nashville: B&H Academic, 2010.

———. *Studying the Historical Jesus.* Grand Rapids: Baker, 2002.

Bock, Darrell L., and Daniel B. Wallace. *Dethroning Jesus: Exposing Popular Culture's Quest to Unseat the Biblical Christ.* Nashville: Thomas Nelson, 2007.

Craig, William Lane. *On Guard.* Colorado Springs: David C. Cook, 2010.

Deissman, Adolf. *Light from the Ancient East.* Translated by Lionel R. M. Strachan. Grand Rapids: Baker, 1965.

Evans, Craig A. *Holman QuickSource Guide to the Dead Sea Scrolls.* Nashville: Holman Reference, 2010.

Feinberg, John S. "1 Peter 3:18–20, Ancient Mythology, and the Intermediate State." *Westminster Theological Journal* 48 (1986): 303–36.

Finegan, Jack. *Handbook of Biblical Chronology.* Rev. ed. Peabody, MA: Hendrickson, 1998.

Fruchtenbaum, Arnold G. *Jesus Was a Jew.* San Antonio: Ariel Ministries, 2010.

———. *Messianic Christology.* Tustin, CA: Ariel Ministries, 1998.

George, Timothy. *Is the Father of Jesus the God of Muhammad?* Grand Rapids: Zondervan, 2002.

Green, Joel B., Scot McKnight, and I. Howard Marshall, eds. *Dictionary of Jesus and the Gospels.* Downers Grove, IL: InterVarsity Press, 1992.

Groothius, Douglas. *Jesus in an Age of Controversy.* Eugene, OR: Harvest House, 1996.

Grudem, Wayne. "Christ Preaching Through Noah: 1 Peter 3:19–20 in the Light of Dominant Themes in Jewish Literature." *Trinity Journal* 7:2 (Fall 1986): 3–31.

Habermas, Gary R. *The Historical Jesus: Ancient Evidence for the Life of Christ.* Joplin, MO: College Press, 1996.

———. *The Secret of the Talipot Tomb: Unravelling the Mystery of the Jesus Family Tomb.* Nashville: Broadman & Holman, 2007.

Hannah, John D. *Our Legacy: The History of Christian Doctrine.* Colorado Springs: NavPress, 2001.

Henry, Carl F. H. *Christian Countermoves in a Decadent Culture.* Portland, OR: Multnomah, 1986.

———. *The Identity of Jesus of Nazareth.* Nashville: Broadman, 1992.

Hindson, Edward E. *Isaiah's Immanuel.* Phillipsburg, NJ: Presbyterian and Reformed Publishing, 1978.

Hitchcock, Mark, and Thomas Ice. *Breaking the Apocalypse Code: Setting the Record Straight About the End Times.* Costa Mesa, CA: Word for Today, 2007.

Hoehner, Harold W. *Chronological Aspect of the Life of Christ.* Grand Rapids: Zondervan, 1977.

House, H. Wayne. *Charts of Christian Theology & Doctrine.* Grand Rapids: Zondervan, 1992.

————. *Chronological and Background Charts of the New Testament.* 2nd ed. Grand Rapids: Zondervan, 2009.

————. *The Jesus Who Never Lived: Exposing False Christs and Finding the Real Jesus.* Eugene, OR: Harvest House, 2008.

House, H. Wayne, and Gordon Carle. *Doctrine Twisting: How Core Biblical Truths Are Distorted.* Downers Grove, IL: InterVarsity Press, 2004.

House, H. Wayne, and Randall Price. *Charts of Bible Prophecy.* Grand Rapids: Zondervan, 2003.

Ice, Thomas, and Timothy J. Demy. *Fast Facts on Bible Prophecy from A to Z.* Eugene, OR: Harvest House, 2004.

Jenkins, Philip. *The Lost History of Christianity.* San Francisco: HarperOne, 2008.

Josephus, Flavius. *Antiquities of the Jews.*

Khalidi, Tarif, ed. and trans. *The Muslim Jesus: Sayings and Stories in Islamic Literature.* Cambridge, MA: Harvard University Press, 2001.

LaHaye Tim, and Thomas Ice, eds. *The End Times Controversy: The Second Coming Under Attack.* Eugene, OR: Harvest House, 2003.

Longenecker, Richard N. *Biblical Exegesis in the Apostolic Period.* 2nd ed. Grand Rapids: Eerdmans, 1999.

Maier, Paul. L. *In the Fullness of Time: A Historian Looks at Christmas, Easter, and the Early Church.* San Francisco: HarperCollins, 1991.

Mayhew, Eugene J. *Encyclopedia of Messianic Candidates & Movements in Judaism, Samaritanism and Islam.* St. Clair Shores, MI: Cadieux & Maheux, 2009.

Metzger, Bruce M. *The New Testament: Its Background, Growth, and Development.* Nashville: Abingdon, 1965.

Pelikan, Jaroslav. *Jesus Through the Centuries.* New Haven, NJ: Yale University Press, 1985.

Price, Randall. *Jerusalem in Prophecy.* Eugene, OR: Harvest House, 1998.

Walvoord, John F. *Jesus Christ Our Lord.* Chicago: Moody Publishers, 1969.

_____. *Major Bible Prophecies: 37 Crucial Prophecies That Affect You Today.* Grand Rapids: Zondervan, 1991.

_____. *Prophecy: 14 Essential Keys to Understanding the Final Drama.* Nashville: Thomas Nelson, 1993.

_____. *The Return of the Lord.* Grand Rapids: Zondervan, 1955.

Wilkins, Michael J., and J. P. Moreland, eds. *Jesus Under Fire: Modern Scholarship Reinvents the Historical Jesus.* Grand Rapids: Zondervan, 1995.

About the Authors

H Wayne House is Distinguished Research Professor of Theology, Law, and Culture at Faith Evangelical Seminary in Tacoma, Washington, and an Adjunct Professor of Biblical Studies and Apologetics at Veritas Evangelical Seminary. Formerly he was Associate Professor of Systematic Theology at Dallas Theological Seminary and Professor of Theology and Culture at Trinity Graduate School, Trinity International University, and Professor of Law at Trinity Law School. He has a JD from Regent University School of Law, a ThD from Concordia Seminary, St. Louis, an MA in Patristic Greek from Abilene Christian University, a ThM and MDiv from Western Seminary, and a BA in Classical and Hellenistic Greek from Hardin-Simmons University.

He has been author, coauthor, and editor of over thirty books, author of more than seventy journal and magazine publications, and a contributor to several books, dictionaries, and encyclopedias. Among his many books are *The Nelson Study Bible* (NT editor); *The Battle for God; Charts on Open Theism and Orthodoxy; Charts of World Religions; Charts of Christian Theology and Doctrine; Chronological and Background Charts of the New Testament; Charts of Cults, Sects, and Religious Movements; A Christian View of Law; Restoring the Constitution; The Jesus Who Never Lived; Israel: The Land and the People; God's Message: Your Sermon;* and *Intelligent Design 101.*

Dr. House serves on the board of numerous organizations and served as president of the Evangelical Theological Society (1991). He leads study tours to Israel every year, and on alternate years to Jordan and Egypt, and Turkey and Greece. He has been married to Leta Frances McConnell for forty-three years and they have two grown children, Carrie and Nathan, and five grandchildren. He may be contacted at info@christianstudytours.com for interest in travel to biblical lands. His website is www.hwhouse.com.

Timothy J. Demy has authored and edited more than two dozen books on the Bible, theology, and current issues. He has also contributed to numerous journals, Bible handbooks, study Bibles, and theological encyclopedias. A professor of military ethics at the US Naval War College, he served more than twenty-seven years as a military chaplain in a variety of assignments afloat and ashore with the US Navy, US Marine Corps, and US Coast Guard. He has published and spoken nationally and internationally on issues of war and peace and the role of religion in international relations. He also serves as Adjunct Professor of Theology at Baptist Bible Seminary.

In addition to his theological training, which he received at Dallas Theological Seminary (ThM, ThD), he received the MSt in international relations from the University of Cambridge and MA and PhD degrees from Salve Regina University, where he wrote about C. S. Lewis. He also earned graduate degrees in European history and in national security and strategic studies and was the President's Honor Graduate from the US Naval War College. He is a member of numerous professional organizations, including the Evangelical Theological Society, the Society of Biblical Literature, and is Fellow of the Royal Society of Arts (UK). He and his wife, Lyn, have been married thirty-three years.